# WHISPERS OF HEALING

### Short Stories, Essays, and Poetry on Survival, Boundaries, and Choosing Yourself

Serenite Hope

ISBN: 979-8-9993596-0-5
Cover design and interior layout by Serenite Hope

This book doesn't come with a table of contents.
There's no map. No numbered chapters. No neat beginning,
middle, or end.

Because healing isn't linear.
It's not a staircase or a checklist or a five-step plan. It's a messy,
beautiful, chaotic spiral of trying, failing, hiding, showing up,
crying at stoplights, laughing at inappropriate times, and
somehow... still moving forward.

What you'll find here is a scattered collection of stories, poems,
moments, and gentle reminders—some long, some barely a
breath. Some stitched with humor. Some heavy with silence.
Some I didn't want to write but needed to.

You can read this book in order, or not. You can flip to a random
page when you're falling apart at 3 a.m., or read the whole thing
in one sitting if you're craving something real. There's no wrong
way to move through it—just like there's no wrong way to heal.

This book is not about being fixed.
It's about being honest.

Thanks for being here, messy heart and all.

_Serenite_

ink stains on my hands—
every line I write bleeds out
something I can hold

Dear Future Me,

I'm ten years old right now, and I don't really know who you are yet or what you look like. But I think I know some important things about you already.

I want to tell you about some stuff that happened. Some of it is really hard to write, but I think you need to remember.

Do you remember when I cut my baby sister's hair? It wasn't a big deal to me, but it was to Mommy. She got so angry. She hit me for hours. The neighbor heard everything. But here's what I figured out, even though I'm only ten: she wasn't really hitting me. She was hitting something else. Something from before. Every time her hand came down, I could see it in her eyes—she was hitting all the people who hurt her when she was little, all the times nobody listened to her, all the times she couldn't fight back.

I know that sounds weird for a kid to understand, but I do. I see it so clearly. She's bleeding inside, and I'm like the cloth she uses to stop it.

I wanted to tell you that I tried really hard to hate her. I wanted to so bad. But my brain won't let me. I already know her sadness, and I've known it forever—since before I could even talk in full sentences. And even though she did terrible things, I decided to love her anyway. Not because she deserves it, but because something in me just can't stop. I thought if I loved her enough, maybe she'd get better. Maybe she'd stop hurting.

I know it started with wanting to save my little sister (remember when she ran toward that motorcycle? I held her hand so tight), but really it started with trying to save Mommy from her own pain.

Sometimes I really wish I could just be mean and not care. I wish I could hate people and not feel sorry for them. But I can't. God put something in me that makes me understand people, even when I don't want to. Even when it hurts.
I want you to know that even at ten, I already know how to make people laugh.

When I laugh, I forget about everything bad. I forget that Daddy left when I was three. I forget about watching the same videos over and over because nobody was really watching me. I forget that Grandma said I'm not really Daddy's kid. When I laugh I forget my older sister keeps taking things just because she can, and I let her. When I laugh, I'm not carrying everybody else's problems. I'm just... me.
My laugh is real. It's not fake. It's mine, and nobody can take it away.

I also want to tell you something that might sound strange: I would totally marry someone like me. I know grown-ups say you shouldn't want that, but I don't get why. If I could marry someone who listens the way I do, who remembers little things about people, who asks good questions, who doesn't get mad about dumb stuff—why wouldn't I? I think most people are just scared to look at themselves in the mirror. But I'm not scared of who I am. I hope you're not scared either.

I hope you still laugh a lot. I hope you still choose to love people even when they don't deserve it, because that's who we are. I hope you stopped trying to save everybody, because I'm starting to learn that's not my job. Only God can really save people.

I hope you know that everything that happened to me—to us—made us strong, but it doesn't make us broken. We're not broken. We're whole. We've always been whole, even when everybody around us was falling apart.

I hope you forgave Mommy. Not because she earned it, but because we can't breathe without it. I hope you understand that she was just a walking bruise trying her best, even though her best hurt us so much.

Most of all, I hope you're still you. Still kind. Still funny. Still able to see people's pain without drowning in it. Still believing that love matters, even when it's hard.
I'm proud of you already, even though I haven't met you yet.

Love,
Your 10-year-old self

P.S. - Do we still like blue best? I hope so. And I hope you still wear jeans everywhere, even to bed, because they make me feel safe.

the girl who needed armor became the
woman who hates how it fits

# I Hate Pants!

IT HAPPENED ON a Tuesday, which feels fitting because Tuesdays are the most untrustworthy day of the week. Monday has the decency to be awful. Wednesday is middle-child neutral.

But Tuesday? Sneaky.

I was trying to take off my jeans—jeans I had worn for over 30 years like emotional armor. Not sexy jeans, not soft jeans. Practical. Dense. Heavy like secrets. And suddenly, in the middle of this daily ritual, I snapped. I was yanking one leg off and nearly dislocated a hip. I screamed—not from pain, but from rage. From the sheer absurdity of it.

"I HATE PANTS!" I yelled to absolutely no one.

Not in the cute, quirky "ugh, leggings forever" way. I mean a deep, feral, chest-cracking hatred.

It echoed off the bathroom tiles like an ancient truth.

I stood there, half-naked, tangled in denim, and I laughed. Not a little giggle. A full, head-thrown-back, snort-laced, maniacal laugh that left me breathless. Somewhere between the scream and the snort, I caught my reflection—half-pants, full fury—and thought, Who am I even doing this for?

That's when it hit me. I've spent my entire adult life bound in denim, not because I liked it, but because I once needed it. As a shield. A lock. A way to sleep with both eyes closed, knowing my body had at least one boundary no one could cross without waking me. But I'm not her anymore—the girl who needed jeans to sleep. I'm 40. I own a heating pad, three kinds of tea, and the ability to say "no" out loud without a nervous laugh.

And I hate pants.

Some women hate bras. I hate pants. I hate putting them on. I hate taking them off. I hate the way they lurk on chairs like denim demons, judging me for choosing sweatpants again. I'm all for equal rights, but if the future is female, then the future better have elastic. What's a better option, you ask? I don't know. Maybe a robe. Maybe a toga. Maybe just... freedom. But pants? Pants are not it.

I don't want to survive—I want to breathe. Pants are liars. They promise structure but deliver oppression. They pinch, they bind, they whisper passive-aggressive comments to your thighs. They demand you tuck your belly in like it's smuggling state secrets.

I want to exhale. I want to sit down without adjusting five times like a human origami project. I want to lie flat on the floor without being reminded of every salty carb I've ever loved. I want to stretch my legs in public without the crotch of my jeans staging a protest. I want to leap dramatically onto the couch like a Victorian heroine.

I want to scream into the void. I want to travel—to vanish into a city where no one knows me and I don't have to smile unless I mean it. I want to learn another language, something soft and romantic and unapologetically not English. I want real, trustworthy friends—the kind who don't flinch at silence and know how to sit with sadness. I want to be seen without being studied. I want to wake up excited, not obligated.

I want to write a manifesto that makes someone feel alive. I want to take up the cello and play sad music in the dark just for myself. I want to live in a lighthouse and knit sweaters for cold, ungrateful seals who don't even say thank you.

But most of all—I want to simply pee without a wrestling match.

Is that too much to ask?

I want ease. Softness. Release.

Which—God help me—makes me wonder: should I consider skirts? Dresses? Flowing, breezy garments that swish when I walk and allow my lower half the dignity of movement?

No.

No, no, no.

The thought alone makes me shudder like I'm watching The Exorcist for the first time, head spinning and all.

Maybe this is healing: not a grand epiphany in a field of sunflowers, but a Tuesday night standoff with your own jeans. Not a rebirth, but a quiet revolution.

And maybe freedom is realizing that being safe and being comfortable don't have to be mutually exclusive anymore.

If you've ever yelled at your wardrobe, you're not alone. Maybe your freedom starts with sweatpants—or simply saying, "no more."

# Things I Don't Say Anymore

I DON'T TELL people I cry when I get overwhelmed, that it's not sadness exactly—just too many things trying to fit inside a body that's too small. I used to explain that, once. Now I just leave the room.

I don't talk about the dream I had at eight years old where the house was burning and I saved everyone but myself. That felt like a metaphor before I even knew what the word meant.

I don't say "I need you to stay," even when I do. Especially when I do. It's easier to pretend I'm built for solitude, that I like the echo.

I don't tell people I still rehearse conversations in my head—full, long, winding things I'll never say out loud. I make room for disappointment in every silence. It's like setting a place at the table for a ghost.

I don't say "I trust you" anymore. Not because no one is worthy, but because I once gave that sentence to someone who held it like a weapon.

I don't talk about the way I flinch at kindness, how compliments make me want to run, how I'm always waiting for the catch. Like love is a net and I'm the fish too smart to swim too close.

I don't explain the way certain songs make my hands shake, or how some days I feel like a locked diary with no key in sight.

I don't talk about how long it takes me to answer a message—not because I don't care, but because I overthink every word until it loses all meaning.

I don't tell people I remember everything—every tone shift, every offhand comment, every silence that lasted just a second too long. It's not forgiveness I struggle with, it's forgetting.

I don't admit that I sometimes test people just to see if they'll leave. That I set little traps with my silence. That I hate myself a little every time they fall for them.

I don't say that I envy people who trust easily. That watching them feels like watching birds fly—beautiful, effortless, and completely beyond me.

I don't talk about the version of myself that only exists in my own head— softer, braver, someone who didn't learn to guard her joy like a secret.

I don't mention how I disappear in crowds, not physically, but in a way that feels like sinking beneath the surface while everyone else keeps dancing.

I don't say how loud my thoughts get at night. How they echo in my chest like a second heartbeat I never asked for.

I don't tell people that "I'm fine" is just code for "please don't ask again." That I say it out of habit, not honesty.

I don't say that I still blame myself for things that weren't my fault, that shame has a way of building a home inside you and calling itself truth.

I don't admit that sometimes, I push people away just to see who tries to come back. And when no one does, I tell myself I knew it all along.

It's not that I don't want to be known.
It's that being known once cost me everything.

And I'm still learning how to believe that this time—this time—might be different.

# The Cost of Coming Home

I DIDN'T LEAVE in anger. People imagine those choices erupt in flames—screaming matches, slammed doors, final words like knives thrown in the dark. But when I walked away, it was quiet. So quiet. Like snowfall after midnight. Just me, standing in the hush, deciding not to pick up the phone anymore.

There was no grand declaration. No dramatic escape. Just a slow exhale I'd been holding for years.

I had bent myself into impossible shapes, hoping to be loved right. Shrinking the parts of me that didn't fit the version they found acceptable. Laughing off cruelty. Swallowing shame that was never mine to carry. Telling myself, This is just how family is.

But even love—yes, even blood—has limits when it starts to consume you from the inside out.

And it does. It eats slow. Like rust creeping over iron. Like mold slipping quietly through drywall. It starts in your voice—you stop telling the truth because it always ends in war. Then your spine—you stop standing tall, always bracing for the blow that might come. Then your heart. And that's the cruelest part: when love tangles itself with fear, when guilt starts to taste like loyalty, and you forget the difference between being held and being hurt. That's the kind of love that hollows you out. That costs you sleep. Sanity. The steady thrum of who you used to be.

They weren't monsters. Just broken people bleeding on anyone who got close. I see that now. The pain behind the sharp words. The fear beneath the control. The ache hidden in silence. And I've forgiven them, truly. My chest carries no bitterness. Only a soft sorrow for what could've been, if healing had come sooner.

But forgiveness doesn't mean handing them new pieces of me to break.

I used to believe love meant staying, no matter the toll. That loyalty meant lighting myself on fire to keep the family warm. But love doesn't ask for your extinction. It doesn't require you to vanish just to belong.

So I left.

Not because I stopped loving them. But because, for once, I finally loved myself enough to stop bleeding for them.

It's lonely sometimes. The kind of lonely that presses against your ribs on quiet Tuesday afternoons. No one to celebrate the big moments with. No laughter woven in the strange language only siblings speak. But in that stillness, I've found something else.

Peace.

My own breath. My own voice. I can sit in my home without flinching. Cry without shame. Laugh without edges. Heal in the sunlight without interruption.

I still love them. And maybe—someday—there will be a path back. Not to what was, but to something honest. Something whole. But if that day never comes, that's okay too.

I've placed us all in gentler hands than mine. Hands that know the work of restoration. Hands that met me in the dark silence and whispered, "You were never wrong to leave."

So I stand here, alone, not in anger—but in grace. And every day, I stitch myself back together. Not so they'll understand.

But because I finally do.

This is the cost of coming home.

And yes—I'd pay it again.

# *Get Up*

Someone left you
Someone lied to you
Someone betrayed you
Someone took advantage of you
Someone didn't believe in you
Someone abandoned you
Someone hates you
Someone used you
Someone abused you

I know it hurts
I know you're tired
You just want to rest

You want to *let go* of the pain
You want to *let go* of the suffering
You want to *let go* of the injustice
You want to *let go* of the oppression
You want to *let go* of the **FEAR**

But it's ALWAYS too soon to give up

**Get up**
You CAN
Can't is an illusion
Can't is the weapon of the enemy
**Get up**
When it hurts to even just breathe
**Get up**

When your knees buckle beneath the weight

**Get up**

When the mirror shows a stranger's face

**Get up**

When the voices say you're not enough

**Get up anyway**

Because you are still here

And that alone is proof

That something in you refuses to break

**Get up**

Not because it's easy

Not because you're ready

But because staying down

Is exactly what they expected

**Get up**

For the version of you who's waiting on the other side

For the life that's still unwritten

For the strength you didn't know you had

Until you had no choice but to find it

**Get up**

Because giving up is permanent

But getting up?

Getting up is always possible

**So get up**

And keep getting up

Until one day

You realize

You're not just standing—

You're walking forward

And then?

You're running.

# Grade Me On A Curve

THEY TOLD ME I was lucky.

"Miracle," one nurse said, like she was trying to sell me a time-share in gratitude.

I heard the word so much in the ICU, it stopped sounding like anything. Just a soft grunt of disbelief people made when they looked at me—then immediately away, like my face was a car crash and they'd already seen one of those this week.

Now, in the bathroom mirror, under the yellow bathroom light that makes everyone look a little sick, I stare at what's left of me. I used to have a symmetrical face. One of those effortlessly pretty ones that got me free drinks and too much attention. Now, half of it is melted like wax. Skin like riverbed mud. A crooked lip that always makes me look half amused, which, today, is finally accurate.

Because here's the thing—I didn't die. Whatever flaming cosmic joke tried to take me out missed. That feels important.

I lean closer. My left eye—still mine, still green—meets itself in the mirror. "You're a ten," I say out loud, "if we're grading on a curve and everyone else is dead."

I laugh. It hurts. The skin tightens in places that used to stretch. But it feels good.

This face? It's proof. Proof I was in the fire. That I crawled out. That I can still laugh, even if it sounds like I've been smoking for forty years.

That I can still feel, even if the nerves disagree.

I don't know what happens next. But I'm done trying to mourn a face that got me attention and not much else.

This one gets me silence,

space,

and very real conversations.

**Honestly,**
it might be an upgrade.

# Turns Out They're People

THEY TELL YOU kids will change your life. What they don't tell you is that the biggest change comes the moment you realize your kids aren't you. They're not mini-me's, not appendages or legacy-projects. They are their own little messes of flesh and spirit and thought—sometimes irritating, sometimes awe-inspiring, but always, undeniably, separate.

It hit me on a Tuesday, which feels unfair. Tuesdays are already struggling to be liked.

I was standing in the kitchen, covered in maple syrup that wasn't mine, staring at my toddler, who was fully naked except for one sock, holding a doll by its foot and declaring, "She doesn't want pants. You don't understand her journey."

And I didn't.

Not just the doll's journey. His. My son. I realized in that moment: he wasn't malfunctioning. He wasn't being difficult. He was just…being him. And I didn't understand him because I had never really tried. I'd been treating parenting like software updates—install discipline, apply rules, reboot at bedtime.

But that's not what this was. These weren't machines. These were people.

I have three of them.

The teenager, Riley, is a fortress of sarcasm and headphones.

For years, I mistook eye-rolling for disrespect, not emotional self-preservation. The other night, I walked past her room and heard crying. Not loud sobs. Just the kind of quiet, leaky crying you do when you're trying to breathe through it. I didn't know if it was over a friend, or a boy, or just the general soul-squish of being fifteen. I knocked, offered my stupid Dad Joke of the Day, and she actually laughed through tears.

That laugh hurt more than any tantrum ever had. Because I realized she was suffering silently to protect me. To not make it my problem. Because somewhere, somehow, I'd taught her I wasn't safe for her truth unless it came in smiles or sarcasm.

I apologized. I don't remember my exact words, but I remember how her whole body relaxed, just for a second, like someone finally opened a window in a stale room.

The tween, Noah, is nine and obsessed with space. He knows more about black holes than I know about taxes. The other day, he came home from school upset. Some kid told him space wasn't real—or something equally idiotic—and I, being the fixer I am, launched into a lecture about how the kid was wrong and how to ignore bullies and how reality is science and feelings are not facts, and—

He just shook his head. "Dad," he said, "I don't need you to explain it. I just wanted you to say it sucks."

It did suck. So I said so. And then we ate cereal for dinner and watched some weird astronaut anime together, and I let him explain wormholes in a way that made me feel like a wormhole was forming in my brain.

I used to think parenting was shaping kids into decent humans. But it turns out, a lot of it is unlearning the nonsense I picked up as a kid.

My own dad once told me, "Kids don't get opinions until they pay bills."

I remember asking why we couldn't get a cat, and he said, "Because I said so, and that's the end of it." It always was. That was the tone of my childhood: authority without explanation, correction without connection. I didn't realize how much it stunted me until I saw myself doing the same thing—until I saw the fear in my daughter's silence, or the way Noah braced before telling me something.

I don't want to be a copy-paste of my father. I don't want to parent with a rubber stamp.

The toddler—Theo—is still small enough to think the word "butt" is peak comedy. And honestly, I agree. But even he has layers. He brings me books about trucks and bees and kids in wheelchairs and asks, "Why?" a hundred times a day. Not to be annoying. (Well, maybe a little.) But mostly because he believes I know things, and he believes that because, so far, I haven't made him feel stupid for asking.

It's a fragile trust, and it's mine to break. I don't want to.

My wife once told me that growing them inside her wasn't some magical soul-bond thing—it was mostly just exhausting. But still, she made them. With her body. Fed them with her bones and blood. I've always envied that. I thought maybe that's why she seemed to understand them better.

But now I know—I can connect too. Not through biology, but by choice. Through presence. Through apology. Through just listening without always trying to correct or convert or contain.

They're not mine to just mold. They're mine to witness, to guide if they let me, and to love.

That realization didn't come with a parade or a TED Talk moment. It came with syrup in my beard and a naked child defending a pantless doll.

15

And somehow, in that chaos, I felt something soft crack open in my chest.

Healing doesn't always show up with fireworks. Sometimes, it arrives in a sticky kitchen, where you finally see your kids for the first time—not as echoes of you, but as the fully formed, baffling, wonderful humans they've been all along.

# Rhythm? Never Met Her.

They say, "Dance like no one's watching,"
But let's be real—they are, and they're judging.
So why not give them a show to recall?
Trip over your shoelace, then moonwalk the fall!

I've got two left feet and a questionable beat,
My rhythm's more "oops" than it is elite.
But still, I shimmy like I've got a plan,
(Though my hips and elbows don't quite understand.)

I twirl like a blender left on high,
And occasionally poke someone right in the eye.
But hey, if laughter's the sound that follows,
Then I'll dance through the day and all of tomorrow.

Because dancing, my friend, is not just for pros,
It's for those with wild hearts and crooked toes.
It's for those who boogie in socks on wet floors,
And slide into cabinets and refrigerator doors.

Today I danced in the cereal aisle—
Got applause from a toddler and a cashier's smile.
So I'm tossing you rhythm, no pressure, no test,
Just bring your own chaos and hope for the best.

The world is absurd—let's meet it halfway,
With a wiggle, a bounce, and a sassy plié.
Your body remembers what your mind forgot:
That joy is a choice, not something you're taught.
So don't stand there still, stuck in your stance...

I dare you. I double dare you.
Will you dance?

# The Art of Letting Go

To want is to tether,
To bind heart and breath to a fleeting star,
Its light shimmering, cold and bright,
always beyond reach,
Yet the thread cuts deep,
Leaving scars where dreams once nestled,
a phantom ache.

I have clasped what I cherished,
Knuckles white, palms blistered.
Desire, a fire that warms
With stolen embers, until it devours—
And then the ashes
Turn heavy in my chest.

There are things too weighty to hold,
Though my soul aches to embrace them,
A hollow yearning in its deepest seams.
A silent storm within, then clarity's soft plea:
"To hold too tight is to lose entirely."
If love, if hope, if longing
Should drain the life it seeks to feed,
Then I must learn the art of release—
The wisdom of open hands.

This is no act of weakness.
It is strength to gaze upon the beauty
Of what I must let go, its fleeting grace,
To whisper, "You are not mine to keep."
Like leaves surrendered to the autumn breeze,
And in this quiet act of surrender,
There is power.
There is peace.

For as I release, I find myself lighter,
Untethered from a battle I could not win.
What stays is choice,
What lingers is breath, a steady flow.
What remains
Is me—whole
And free.

# Healing Them, Breaking Me

THE INK BLOOMS on the paper, threading itself into the delicate ridges of the baby's palm. A map to somewhere they will never go, a destination I will never reach. I lift the handprint into the light, watching it settle, an echo of existence, fragile and irretrievable.

A hat rests beside shoes too small to have ever met the ground, their softness still thick with absence. A blanket lies untouched, its folds as crisp and sterile as the room around us—silent, waiting for warmth that will never come. I place them gently into the box, as though gathering fragments of a dream that woke too soon, too soon.

The mother cradles her child the way sorrow cradles time—gentle, relentless, refusing to let go. Her hands tremble, but she wills them still. The weight of her grief presses against my chest, more familiar than I want it to be. The father stands apart, arms crossed, grief pulling him inward like the ocean at low tide, retreating into itself.

No one speaks. Loss does not need words to be understood.

I tell myself I've been trained for this. That my hands won't shake. That my breath will steady itself, that I am here to hold space, to bear witness. But grief does not care for repetition. It slips under skin, settles into bones, curls itself into the spaces between ribs. It lives in the weight of remembering.

I reach for the scissors.

And then I hesitate.

My fingers go cold. Time stretches thin, like a thread pulled taut.

They never prepare you for this part. Not in the books, not in the training. There's no module on how to hold steady when the air is thick with goodbye, no checklist for how to sever something so impossibly sacred. I wonder—if I had known this was part of it, really known—would I still have chosen this life?

The mother leans in close, smoothing the baby's hair with the gentlest touch I've ever witnessed. She whispers something only he will hear, words too soft to reach my ears but loud enough to echo in my heart. There's a kind of peace in her voice, a thread of love that refuses to break, even now.

And just like that, I know.

Yes. I would still choose this.

Because this work—this quiet, soul-shaking work—is not just something I do. It's something I am.

The scissors glide through the lock of hair, too easily, like cutting through water. Strands that should have danced in the wind—fragile, irreplaceable, unbearably final. I smooth them between my fingertips and place them carefully into the box. They seem too light. Too small.

The lid closes with a slow, deliberate click. The sound is sharp and final, like a door shutting behind me.

I breathe.

But grief stays with me.

It lingers in my hands, in the hum of the lights above, in the sterile, clean scent that clings to everything. I do not speak of it. No one does. But it follows, like the faintest whisper of a name I will never say again.

Healing is never loud. It arrives in small offerings, in the brief exchange of a glance, in hands that remember, in love that does not fade.

And in the silence, between the weight of loss and the weight of memory, something shifts. Something tender unfolds, small and fleeting. It is not for them. It is not for me.

But for a moment, in the stillness, I feel it. The briefest touch of healing —not for what has been lost, but for the tenderness that lives in the spaces we leave behind.

For the love that persists even when there is no heartbeat.

I carry it with me.

And I wonder if it will be enough to carry me too.

# Green Light

THE ROAD HOME is empty enough that I don't have to focus. Just the hum of tires on asphalt and the rhythmic flash of streetlights across the wind-shield. He's asleep beside me, head tilted awkwardly toward the window, mouth slightly open. He looks smaller like this. Human, almost.

His hands—those same ones that once slammed doors and never quite knew how to hold softness—rest in his lap, the IV tape still wrapped around the crook of his arm. I remember those hands as monsters. Now they tremble when he reaches for the thermostat.

It's stupid, but I turned the radio off before we left. I didn't want to miss it if he said something. Anything. But now he's quiet, and the quiet fills me. It pours into the spaces I've kept sealed for decades. The little girl who waited for apologies that never came. Who learned to be small, to dodge, to anticipate.

I stare straight ahead and feel my face twist before the tears come. I don't sob. I don't wail. I just cry—quietly, steadily—as if something inside me has finally been given permission. Not because he said sorry. He never will. But because he needs me now. Because I'm doing it anyway.

Because tenderness, even when it comes too late, is still tenderness.

The light turns green, and I keep driving.

# Echoes in the Quiet

In the stillness, where love should linger,
I find its absence like a hollow singer.
No tender hands to chase the ache,
No hearts that warm, no bonds to make.

I stand alone in this shadowed plain,
Familiar with loss, acquainted with pain.
Yet still, my soul, with defiant light,
Chooses love—unseen, but bright.

I know the weight of love denied,
The yearning pulse that can't be satisfied.
To feel unloved, uncared for—cold,
Yet clutch the warmth my own heart holds.

I walk a path where dreams must yield,
No children's laughter in my field.
And though my arms may not embrace
A child of mine, I leave my trace.

For every child I meet, I'll be
A fleeting source of love, carefree.
Though just a moment, short and sweet,
I'll give my all in our heartbeat.

Yet love, so freely given, bare,
Becomes a gift some strip and tear.
They take my kindness, carve their gain,
Leaving me wary, nursing the pain.

I hesitate, my walls arise,
A shield between my heart and lies.
But still, the spark within me yearns,
For true connection, my soul returns.

I laugh at life, the irony deep,
And cry for all the dreams I keep.
For though I walk this lonely trail,
My love for others will not pale.

I sow the seeds in barren ground,
For those who hurt, for hearts unwound.
And though my harvest may not bloom,
I'll scatter hope through winter's gloom.

So here I stand, with arms wide-spread,
A lantern lit where none have tread.
I may not feel what others do,
But I'll love the world; I'll love for two.

# Shoelaces

THE FRONT DOOR sticks. I yank it harder than I need to and it shudders in its frame. My backpack thuds against my side.

I'm already late.

"Hold up," Grandpa says from the hallway. "Your laces."

I glance down. One shoe is tight, the other looped in a crooked knot I didn't double. I groan. "It's fine."

But he's already kneeling, slow and stiff, his knees cracking like dry branches. His hands hover for a second before reaching out. I flinch, just a little, then let them.

His fingers are thick, callused. He ties the knot carefully—balanced, neat. Loops tucked just right. He used to do this when I was five and couldn't figure it out. Before I learned to do everything myself. Before the silence between us grew long and full of things we never talked about.

I glance down. His head is bowed, his white hair soft and thin. He doesn't say anything. Just pulls the laces snug and gives them a gentle tug like he used to, like it means something.

And maybe it does.

Maybe this is his way of saying what he never says. That he's sorry. That he sees me. That he still wants to show up, even if he doesn't know how to say it out loud.

He pats my shin once, then stands with effort. "There," he says. "Now you won't trip."

I nod. I don't say thank you. But I don't pull away.

I step outside into the cold, my shoes tied just right. Tight enough to hold. Loose enough to move.

A lot happened that day. I don't remember most of it.

But I remember the knot.
I remember the quiet.
I remember that it held.

# You are Already Enough.

Your worth isn't tied to productivity,
perfection, or validation from others.
Accept yourself as you are, and remind yourself daily
that you are whole, even while healing or growing.

# Still You, Still Me

CLARA STOOD IN the middle of the living room, fingers tracing the edge of James's favorite armchair—the one that had lost a battle with gravity multiple times thanks to his "intense lounging technique." The silence was loud. Not like a peaceful yoga-silence, but more like the silence that follows a vacuum cleaner abruptly turning off in the middle of an argum-ent. Her eyes drifted shut, chasing the sound of his laugh, the feel of his warm, always-too-hot embrace. Time outside marched on, but inside, hers was still negotiating a truce with grief.

Their love story was legendary—or at least it would be, once she figured out how to write a TikTok video about it. Clara and James had known each other since the days of scraped knees and lopsided pigtails. They married young, mostly because they couldn't imagine waiting to have a lifetime of inside jokes. James had always treated her like royalty, and by royalty, she meant he insisted on fluffing her pillows, did 98% of the cooking, and once actually installed a bidet for "her majesty's comfort."

So, naturally, when she found herself alone, the reality hit hard: she didn't know how to unclog a drain, use their overly fancy espresso machine, or even find the warranty folder (James had labeled it "The Scrolls of Destiny"). Still, grief gave her a crash course in adulting. She celebrated the small wins: like learning to change a light bulb without a YouTube tutorial—or only watching half of one.

Then one evening, while trying to Marie Kondo her way through James's things, Clara found a weathered leather journal tucked into a drawer. It smelled like his cologne—equal parts cedarwood and "I refused to throw this shirt away because it still smells like him."

Her hands trembled as she flipped it open.

Inside were reflections, thoughts, and dreams. She learned James had once seriously considered opening a grilled cheese food truck. ("It would've been called Holy Smokes, That's Cheese!") But among the laughter were letters—dozens of them—all addressed to her. Some were profound, others featured doodles of her with giant eyes and freakishly long eyelashes.

One letter hinted at a "treasure," a surprise James had cooked up before his final goodbye. And just like that, curiosity shoved grief aside and hollered, "Adventure time!"

Her first stop was the old bookstore—their shared sanctuary. The place still smelled of old paper and roasted beans, with dust motes floating like they were auditioning for a slow-motion film. While browsing, a book quite literally leapt from the shelf.

It was her poetry book. The one she had emotionally yeeted out of her life during the Grief Rage Phase—right between the "crying on the floor" and "eating cheese straight from the block" phases. She had donated it deliberately, almost defiantly, thinking, If I don't get to keep James, I don't get to keep anything I love. Melodramatic? Absolutely. But poetic, in a falling-apart-on-a-Tuesday kind of way.

As she flipped through the familiar pages of the poetry book, Clara's fingers paused on something fragile. Pressed delicately between the leaves was a flower—dried, delicate, and somehow still vibrant. It marked the very spot of the last poem she had read to James at his bedside.

"In the quiet of the night, our hearts find their true home," she whispered, her voice barely above breath. The words hovered, soft as memory.

Reading to James had been their ritual in those final days. Even when words failed him, her voice—calm and steady, wrapped around verses—was the only thing that seemed to soothe him. She remembered the way his hand had curled around hers, his expression softening as she spoke, their connection clinging to every line.

Her fingers trembled as she traced the flower's edges, the petals like echoes of their last shared moments. It was such a small thing, but in that moment, it was everything.

And then came the kicker: a note scribbled in his handwriting—**"For Clara, my eternal muse. Keep reading, keep dreaming."** She clutched the book to her chest, tears mixing with the smell of nostalgia and bookstore air freshener.

She nearly walked into a wall on the way out, distracted and emotional, only to be intercepted by Sarah.

"Clara! Fancy meeting you here," Sarah said, like this wasn't part of an elaborate, grief-defying plot.

Later, at their favorite café, the air was rich with the familiar hum of clinking cups and the hiss of steamed milk. Emma, her favorite barista, floated over without even asking. A heart-shaped foam smiled up at Clara from her latte.

"Just the way you like it," Emma said, as if nothing in the world had changed—even though everything had.

Clara found another note from James under a sugar jar:
**"Roses are red, violets are blue, you always drink most of my coffee, but I still love you. Clara, my mornings are usually short on coffee but incomplete without you. I hope this note brings a smile to your face, just as you always do for me. Love, James."**

She snorted into her latte. James was romantic in a dad-joke poet laureate kind of way. The audacity of him to call her out like this even from the grave was so typical of him. James always knew how to make her smile. She could almost hear his voice, teasing yet tender.

David showed up too, because apparently, fate (and group chats) wanted her to heal in the company of her favorite people. "Missed our chats," he said, and for once, that didn't make her sad.

At the park, where they used to sit on "their bench" (left side for her, right side for James—non-negotiable), she found an old photo tucked in the armrest. She sat down, gave his spot a pat like he might magically appear, and blinked back tears.

"Clara, is that you?" came Emily's voice, mid-walk with her dog Max— who immediately tried to eat a leaf and then her shoelace. "Mind if we crash your moment?"

"You? Mind? Ha. Pull up a bench."

The final clue led her to the lake—their lake—where sunsets always looked like they were painted just for them. Beneath an ancient oak was a small wooden box. Inside was a locket with their wedding photo. She clutched the locket to her heart. In that moment, she felt James's presence more strongly than ever. She realized that while he was no longer physically with her, his love would always be a part of her.

But then, like the universe was tired of being serious, her phone buzzed. Unknown number: "Look inside the locket."
Which was… mildly threatening? But she did. And tucked inside it (how, she would never understand, James must've had locket-folding superpowers) was a note. Again. Which meant—**wait**. Who was texting her?

**"Our love is eternal, and so is your strength. This is not the end, my love. Follow your heart, live fully, and you'll find me in every step you take."**

She ugly-cried, the kind of cry where you make sounds you hope no one ever records.

Months later, Clara was hosting a sunny lunch at home, having graduated from Instant Ramen to "cooks salmon without setting off the smoke alarm." Her garden bloomed like her soul was finally catching its breath. Surrounded by her friends, she raised a glass. "I wouldn't have made it without you all. And that treasure hunt? Pure magic. James really outdid himself."

Everyone exchanged glances.

"Okay, so… minor plot twist," Sarah said. "James had some help."

David smiled softly. "We took turns following you to each location. Made sure you'd find everything exactly as James wanted. And if it looked like you needed support... we 'accidentally' bumped into you."

Clara blinked, then laughed through fresh tears. "I knew it wasn't a coincidence. What, were you all in some kind of grief ninja squad?"

Sarah popped around the corner mid-chip-crunch, unapologetically unbothered. "Ninja? Please. I was a wizard. That book that flew off the shelf? That was me. I sneezed so hard I thought I'd astral projected. Guinness is still reviewing the footage for the world's longest sneeze, by the way."

Emily raised her hand sheepishly. "And that creepy message about looking inside the locket? Yeah... that was me. Auto-correct was my nemesis. It kept changing 'look inside the locket' to 'look inside the socket' then 'cook inside the rocket.' You nearly went on a space mission with a spatula, girl! I nearly walked into a lamppost trying to fix it!"

The room dissolved into laughter—real, messy, healing laughter. And in that moment, surrounded by the ridiculous, beautiful people who refused to let her grieve alone, Clara knew something sacred: grief had changed her, yes—but it hadn't broken her. Love, the kind she and James shared, left marks on the soul that didn't fade. It lingered in pressed flowers, in lattes topped with hearts, in poorly autocorrected texts, and in the absolute absurdity of healing.

# The Edge of Grief

I do not know your sorrow's name,
nor the weight of who you lost,
but I can hear the silence you carry
like a hymn with no sound.

I stand beside it, not inside it—
no footprints in your storm—
just watching the sky you live beneath
collapse in a different form.

You hold their name like broken glass,
and I, with empty hands,
can only offer the stillness
of someone who understands.

Not the pain—but the shape of it.
Not the loss—but the truth of love,
how it carves us open
and leaves behind echoes.

So I won't say "I know."
I won't try to mend or move.
I will stay where grief hums low,
a witness to the bruise.

Because sometimes, the kindest thing
is not to fix or flee—
but to stand at the edge of someone's sorrow
and say, "I see."

# January 15

The Silence Wasn't Empty.

We sat there, side by side, not touching. The porch boards creaked beneath us like they were trying to speak the things we wouldn't.

The fight hadn't been loud, but it had left its mark—edges sharpened, breath uneven. I could still feel the last words hanging in the air between us, stale and heavy.

And then we just... stopped. No apology. No tidy ending. Just twenty minutes of watching the wind tug at the trees, of sipping lukewarm tea we forgot we were holding.

I didn't look at you, but I felt your breath even out beside me. I let mine follow.

A shared exhale.

A truce without terms.

Something eased in that quiet. Not fixed, not forgotten.
But softened.

And somehow, that was enough—for now.

# The Overflowing Heart

You cannot pour from emptiness,
Cannot give what you don't possess.
To love the world with open hands,
First learn to meet your own demands.

A well runs dry when drawn too deep,
When all you give, you never keep.
But fill yourself—with rest, with care—
And suddenly there's more to spare.

The overflow, unbidden, spills,
It moves through valleys, over hills.
Compassion comes without the strain
When your own cup is full again.

So tend yourself with gentle grace,
Give your own heart its rightful place.
The more you honor what's inside,
The wider love becomes, the stronger its tide.

# Receipt #143

THE SCANNER BEEPS a slow rhythm, steady and impersonal. I slide cans, boxes, a loaf of rye bread across the glass, watching the numbers tally up on the screen like they always do—silent, exact, unfeeling.

It's hour six of a long shift, and my name tag itches against my collar. No one really looks at me. They hand me their things, their cards, sometimes a crumpled coupon, and take their bags without a word. I try to smile. It doesn't always stick.

He's next in line. Thin, a little hunched, moving with careful intention. A brown cardigan, buttoned all the way up. He sets his groceries down with a soft clatter: tea, tissues, a small bottle of honey. Nothing heavy. Nothing hurried.

When I greet him, he looks right at me—not through me—and says, "Well now, aren't you a bright spot today."

It catches me off guard. I almost laugh, but I don't. I just smile, and this time, it's real.

His voice is gentle, the kind that makes you want to lean in closer without knowing why. He watches me ring up his items like it's an art form. Like it matters.

"My granddaughter's about your age," he says, as I bag the honey. "She's always rushing. The world moves too fast now."

I nod, not sure what to say, but he's not really asking for an answer.

When the receipt prints, curling like smoke from the machine, I hand it to him with practiced ease. "Receipt number 143," I say, before I even think.

He takes it with a smile. "Now that's a special one," he says, tapping the number. "Means more than most people remember."

I raise an eyebrow, curious, but he just chuckles, not giving anything away.

"Keep doing what you're doing," he says, folding it neatly, "You've got a good way about you."

The words are small. Simple. But they land somewhere deep—beneath the fluorescent lights and the corporate apron and the tired rhythm of the day.

I watch him walk away, slow but steady, receipt tucked in his pocket like something worth keeping.

The next customer steps forward, setting down a gallon of milk and a pack of gum. She glances after him, then looks at me.
"143," she says with a small smile. "It's code for 'I love you.' You know, one letter, four letters, three letters."

I blink, suddenly still. My hands hover over the register.

And for the first time in a long time, I don't feel invisible. I don't feel lesser.

I feel seen.

Just enough to matter.

# Tapestry of Time and Tears

A whisper in the mirror, "Are you enough?"
The judging eyes that linger, feeling rough.
Will the boys ever notice? Will the girls ever care?
A constant, gnawing worry in the fragile air.
The fear of being different, a stain upon the soul,
Of not quite fitting the prescribed, controlling role.
Her body picked apart, his silence made a mask—
Each trying to belong, a never-ending task.
Each image, each comment, a sting or a dare,
A desperate yearning for acceptance hanging in the air.

The future stretches, vast and terrifyingly wide,
Which path to choose, where should ambition hide?
Will love arrive like in the fairy tales they told?
Or will I walk this journey, forever feeling cold?
She's told to chase dreams, but not too far or fast,
He's told to never cry, to always make it last.
The pressure to succeed, to earn and to provide,
While a quiet voice inside whispers, "Can I run or hide?"
The fear of wrong turns, of hopes that disappear,
Of being left behind, year after relentless year.

The ticking clock, a phantom at the door,
"When will you settle down? What are you waiting for?"
The wedding bells are chiming, a societal demand,
A ring upon the finger, a life within their hand.
But what if independence still burns within the chest?

What if this path feels borrowed, not what's truly best?
She's called too picky, he's told to make the move,
But neither feels quite ready to find a perfect groove.
The fear of being single, a label whispered low,
Of missing out on something all the "grown-ups" seem to know.

The gentle swell beneath the heart, a longed-for, precious dream,
But what if nature falters? What if it doesn't seem?
For her, a ticking womb; for him, a quiet ache,
Wondering if it's selfish to dream of what they can't make.
The scales of work and parenting, a tightrope walked with grace,
Each wondering if they're falling behind in some grand race.
The guilt, the sacrifice, the never-ending stuff—
The fear of being present, yet never quite enough.
And in the quiet moments, a flicker in the glass,
The first faint lines appearing, time moving on too fast.

The vibrant bloom begins to subtly fade,
A frantic search for remedies, a silent, desperate raid
On creams and potions, workouts and disguise,
While youth slips softly through disbelieving eyes.
Her children grow and pull away, a bittersweet release,
His career slows down, and silence replaces peace.
Who am I now, with less to chase or prove?
The fear of being useless, with nothing left to move.
Of being invisible, no longer in the race—
Of losing all their worth in this shifting, aging place.

The body shifts, a landscape rearranged,
Hormones rage or fade, and everything feels changed.
The empty nest echoes, a poignant, hollow sound,
Have we fulfilled our purpose? Has meaning been found?
He aches in joints once strong,
she mourns the youthful glow,
Both learning how to bend without letting go.
The whispers of retirement, a slowing of the pace,
But the spirit still feels vibrant, longing for its place.
The fear of fading out, of being put out to pasture,
While a fierce, resilient soul still yearns for something faster.

The mirror reflects stories etched upon each face,
Each line a memory, a moment they embrace.
But shadows lengthen, health becomes a fragile thing,
And loss, a constant companion, its mournful song will sing.
She dreads becoming burdensome, he fears losing control,
The creeping fade of memory, the tremble in the soul.
The world moves on so quickly, a dizzying, rapid spin,
Will we be left behind, with nowhere to begin?

The years have piled like autumn leaves, a tapestry of time,
I see the young me I was, in this aging paradigm.
The fears still linger, softened by the passing tide,
But wisdom whispers louder, with nothing left to hide.
The fear of final moments, a natural, human dread,
But also gratitude for the life that I have led.
For all the battles fought, the joys I held so dear,
And though the echoes fade, a peaceful strength is here.

# Chipped Nail Polish

SHE WAS SLEEPING when I came in.
Thin blanket pulled up to her waist, hands resting on top—still, except
for the faint twitch of a dream in her fingers.
That's when I noticed it.

Red polish, chipped at the edges.
Worn down to the beds.
Like it had once meant something.
Like it still did.

Later, when I helped her sit up and offered water, I mentioned it gently.
"Nice color," I said, brushing a fingertip near hers. "It's almost gone."

She looked down at her hands, and for the first time that day, she smiled.

"My daughter did them," she said. "A few weeks ago. Or maybe longer.
She always hated when I let them go dull."

There was a pause, and then—almost shyly—she added,
"Do you have any polish?"

I didn't. But I found some.
A bottle left behind in a drawer at the nurse's station—red, just a little
brighter than hers. I brought it back, unsure if it was silly, or if someone
would say it wasn't worth the time.

But she lit up when she saw it.
Held out her hands like they still remembered being held.

We sat together, her hands resting in mine, warm and delicate and flecked
with sunspots and time.
I painted slowly. Carefully.
Not because it needed to be perfect,
but because I wanted it to feel like care.

She told me about her favorite shade of lipstick.
About dancing in high heels.
About being looked at, once, like she was something rare.

And I realized then:
This—this quiet ritual of color and closeness—
was healing too.

No chart for it.
No prescription.
Just two people, sitting in the soft space between roles,
where one is seen, and the other learns how deep care can go.

When I finished, she turned her palms upward, admiring the shine.

"Lovely," she whispered.

And it was.

Because sometimes,
the most human parts of this job
have nothing to do with medicine at all.

# After the Scream

THE FLUORESCENT LIGHTS hum above as I sit at the bar, the laminated menu sticky at the edges, my reflection caught in a row of liquor bottles. Honey garlic chicken, shrimp fried rice. Easy choices. Comfort food, familiar in a world that suddenly feels unfamiliar. The server's voice breaks through the static in my head—bright, polite, utterly unaware of the storm clawing beneath my skin. I smile. I answer. Inside, I am howling. Every word is a betrayal of the scream lodged in my throat like broken glass.

The air feels too thick as I make my way back to the car. My hands tremble on the steering wheel. I am swallowing it, over and over— this terrible, raw noise that wants to break through. A scream not of rage, not of hunger, but of something else, older, darker, harder to name. Grief? Emptiness? Maybe just the weight of being.

The absurdity of it all—waiting for takeout and wanting to erupt. But the scream has grown teeth now. I drive. Five minutes. Then ten.

And I let go.

It tears out of me—not like the movies, no graceful soprano of horror—but a deep, guttural wrench of sound. An animal cry, untranslatable. I do it again. And again. The silence after is heavier, but cleaner. My heart stills. I breathe.

I go home.

I eat my food in peace.

**Healing whispers**
in small moments, carried on breath—
after the scream.

# The Click of a Latch

MY FINGERS HOVER over the doorknob. It's smooth and cold, even in the sweltering heat of the apartment. Outside, cicadas scream like they're burning alive.

Inside, everything is still.

The silence isn't peace. It's the kind that follows slammed doors and hissed insults. The kind that wraps itself around your ribs and tightens when you breathe. My suitcase is at my feet. Half-zipped. Crooked from where I shoved it closed in a panic. I forgot socks. Maybe toothpaste. Doesn't matter.

The floorboards creak behind me. A sound I used to brace for. I glance over my shoulder, but the hallway is empty. He's not home. Not yet. That's the only reason I got this far.

My heart thumps like it's trying to count the seconds before I lose my nerve.

I can still hear his voice, not in the air, but in me.

"No one else will want you."
"You're too sensitive."
"You always ruin things."

His words live here. I don't want to.

I press my palm to the door, lean into it like it might fall open on its own. Outside, a neighbor's dog barks. The sound is sharp, clean. Alive. Something in me stirs.

Then, with both hands, I turn the knob. Slowly. The door opens with a quiet sigh. I step into the hallway. The air smells different—distant cooking, someone's laundry, freedom. My suitcase wheels squeak as I drag it over the threshold.

I pull the door shut behind me. The latch clicks.

Soft.

Final.

I close my eyes and let the sound echo.

It's just a latch.
But it feels like the first time I've ever said *no*.

fear and courage both live in me
only one gets tacos

# Midnight Fridge Light

THE CLOCK SAYS 2:13. I wasn't hungry exactly—just restless.
The kind of quiet that settles too deep in the bones, like the night is holding its breath and waiting for you to notice.

I open the fridge.

The light spills out like a secret. Cold air kisses my skin. I stare at the shelves, half-empty. A jar of olives, a bruised peach, leftovers I won't eat.

I consider the peach. I've been avoiding it for four days because it feels like a commitment.

It feels like a metaphor, but I'm too tired to chase it.

My hand hovers over the milk, then the peach. Then nothing. I just stand there, one foot cold on the tile, the other curled for warmth.

The fridge hums like it's trying to reassure me. Either that or it's plotting. Hard to tell at 2:13.

There's no music. No voice saying, you're okay now. Just the hum of the refrigerator and the sound of my own breathing.

And I realize—I'm not waiting for something to happen anymore. Not tonight. Not from anyone. Just standing here is enough.

I close the door gently.
The darkness returns like an exhale.

# Hangry Games: Family Edition

I HATE RUDENESS. Like, deep in my bones. If someone snaps at me, my tongue usually transforms into a fully-loaded, sarcasm-slicked flamethrower before I can even blink. I'm not proud of it, but I have perfected the art of the clap back. It's a skill I keep sharp—like knives in a drawer labeled "just in case."

So when I called my dad that afternoon—just to remind him of a dentist appointment he insisted I help him remember—I wasn't expecting to need my armor. I was doing a good daughter thing, you know? Community service with a blood bond.

The phone rang twice before he answered with an irritated grunt that sounded like I'd just interrupted his bid for sainthood.
"What?!" he barked. Not a hello. Not a "Hi sweetheart." Just… What.

I blinked. "Uh… hi? Just calling to remind you your appointment's at three. You said to call around now in case you forgot."

Silence for a second. Then, he exploded:
"Well, I'm not going anymore, alright?! I had to change my plans—why are you bothering me with this right now?"

There it was. The spark.

Now, normally? That would've been the moment I reached for the flamethrower. I felt the heat rise up my neck. My brain instantly queued up five spicy comebacks and a dramatic "Excuse me?" with full shoulder choreography—a poetic roast about ungrateful people and bad attitudes.

For a flash of a second, I saw red. Like actual flames.

But then something happened—I paused. Mid-snap, mid-flare, I stopped. Took a breath that probably saved both of our blood pressure numbers.

And I'm not saying I became the Dalai Lama in that moment, but something inside me whispered, "Don't match fire with fire." So I let the silence stretch. Just a few seconds. But long enough for him to hear it. Feel it.

He went quiet too. I could hear him breathing. Like he suddenly realized he'd just shot the messenger for delivering a message he himself had requested.

Then, as calmly as I could, I said, "Hey, it sounds like we're working with different information. I didn't know your plans had changed—I just called because that's what we agreed on."

Still no snap from me. Zero flames. I even surprised myself.

He exhaled like someone had let the air out of a balloon shaped like his pride.

Then I softened the whole thing with a smile in my voice and said, "Wait… have you had lunch yet?"
A small pause.
"No," he grumbled. "I haven't even had coffee."

"Aha. That explains everything," I said. "You're operating under emergency conditions."

He actually laughed—just a little. But enough to know we'd both stepped back from the edge.

We agreed he'd go eat, I'd text instead of call next time, and neither of us had to pretend the rudeness never happened. We just... rerouted it. With food. As all family problems should be.

It was one of those moments where I realized: healing isn't always a grand gesture. Sometimes it's a breath. A beat. A decision to feed someone instead of fight them.

Also, I'm pretty sure hangry is hereditary. So at least now I know where I get it from.

# Set Boundaries and Honour Them.

Know your limits and communicate them clearly.
Boundaries protect your peace, time, and energy—
set them without guilt, and enforce them
with consistency and compassion.

# Butterflies Don't Ask for Applause

"ARIA, MY DEAR, you work too hard! When will you find a nice boy and settle down?"

Mrs. Wong's voice greeted her before Aria could even finish dialing. It was the same question every time she called Wong's Garden— same warmth, same determination to marry her off to David, the Star Wars-obsessed doctor still living in his mother's basement.

"Mrs. Wong, I barely have time to sleep, let alone date," Aria replied, stifling a yawn and a laugh.

"But what about my David? He's a doctor! So smart, so handsome, so hardworking!"

"David? The massive Star Wars nerd who cornered me at your New Year's party to debate the moral complexity of the Jedi Order? He showed me his limited edition Ewok figures like they were ancient artifacts."

"Aria! You say that like it's a bad thing! He is passionate! They're collectibles!" Mrs. Wong said, scandalized. "He's just waiting for the right girl to appreciate Chewbacca's emotional depth to move out!"

"Well, when you find her, I want front row seats to the wedding."

Mrs. Wong sighed dramatically. "The usual, then?"

"Please. Steak and broccoli, shrimp fried rice—"

"And spring rolls. I know, I know. You are too predictable, Aria."

"Predictable keeps me sane, Mrs. Wong."

That call was typical. So was everything else.

Aria's life was a loop—hospital corridors humming with machinery, the bitter aroma of coffee strong enough to wake the dead, the sharp scent of antiseptic, patients clinging to hope with trembling hands. The emotional weight was often heavier than her scrubs after a double shift. There was the sacred art of not sneezing during a sterile procedure. And then there was more coffee, because hope is good, but caffeine is better.

After every shift came the same ritual: call Wong's Garden (check), endure Mrs. Wong's matchmaking (check), walk the ten minutes home waving to the kids at the basketball court ("Use the force, Luke!"), dodge Luna's nightly ankle assassination attempts (the cat had professional-level dedication), collapse into The Throne—her dad's ancient recliner that creaked like a ship but held more emotional support than a therapy group with free snacks—and let SpongeBob SquarePants undo the knots in her chest one absurd episode at a time.

Predictable. Exhausting. Oddly comforting.

Until the letter arrived.

A weathered envelope sat on her doorstep one morning like it had traveled through time and mild rain. Inside, elegant handwriting read:

*"To the one who gives so much, yet asks for so little. Your kindness has not gone unnoticed."*

No name. No clue. Just enough mystery to make her wonder if she'd accidentally wandered into a Hallmark movie.

And that's when everything changed.

***

More letters followed over the next few weeks. Each one referenced moments she had forgotten—or never realized mattered at all.

One mentioned the little boy in the park.

She remembered him now: Tommy, tears streaming down his face, lost and terrified.

"Let's find your mom together, okay? What's your name?"

"Tommy," he sniffled.

"Okay, Tommy. Favorite dinosaur?"

"...Spinosaurus."

"Strong choice. You've got good instincts."

They'd found his mother eventually, frantic and sobbing with relief.

"Thank you," the woman had said, clutching her son like he might disappear again.

"Glad he's safe," Aria had replied with a smile. "He's got a future in paleontology."

She'd forgotten about it the next day. But someone hadn't.

Another letter mentioned the elderly woman on the bench—the one Aria had sat with on a cold, windy night outside the hospital. The woman had been crying quietly, and Aria, exhausted from her shift, had simply sat down beside her.

"Do you want to talk about it?" Aria had asked.

"I just… don't want to be alone tonight."

So Aria had stayed. For an hour. Maybe more. She'd offered her coat, her company, and a packet of tissues from her purse. They'd talked about nothing and everything—about loss, about loneliness, about the little things that keep you going.

The letter said: *"You saved my life that night. I hope you know that."*

Aria's throat tightened as she read it. She hadn't known. She'd just been tired and kind. But to that woman, it had been everything.

Then came a package.

Inside was a silver bracelet with a single butterfly charm, delicate and shimmering. Tucked beneath it, a note: *"Thank you."*
Butterflies.

Her grandmother used to say, "Butterflies are proof you can go through a lot of darkness and still become something beautiful."

Aria stared at the bracelet, her eyes stinging. Whoever was sending these letters knew her. Really knew her. And that thought was equal parts comforting and unsettling.

The next gift was a leather-bound poetry book—Shakespeare, Keats, Frost—with a handwritten poem awkwardly scrawled in the back about coffee and compassion. She didn't know whether to laugh or cry, so she did both while eating spring rolls.

Each page felt like a little healing salve. She'd been holding it together with sarcasm and caffeine, but this? This was nourishment for a part of her she'd been ignoring.

***

Then came the invitation.

Her mother called one morning, voice bright with mischief. "You're coming to the cookout this weekend. No excuses."

"Mom, I have a double shift—"

"You have the day off. I already checked."
Aria blinked. "You called my supervisor?"

"I'm your mother. I have my ways. Be here. Two o'clock. Don't be late."

***

The cookout was pure chaos in the best way. Her mom's grill smoked like it was summoning ancestral spirits. Her dad manned the burgers with the focus of a surgeon. Cousins ran wild. Laughter bounced off the walls.

Aria hadn't realized how much she'd needed this—the noise, the warmth, the reminder that she wasn't just a nurse. She was a daughter, a sister, a friend.

Then her mother tapped a glass, and the chatter quieted.

"I just want to say something," her mom began, looking directly at Aria.

Aria braced herself. This usually meant something embarrassing.

"Aria, your kindness and dedication have touched so many lives. We are so proud of you."

A chorus of applause broke out. Aria blinked, confused, as faces emerged from the crowd—faces she recognized.

Former patients. Old neighbors. The elderly woman from the park bench, eyes wet with gratitude.

She approached Aria slowly, lavender-scented and soft-spoken.

"You saved my life," she whispered. "You sat with me when I had no one. That night changed everything."

Aria's breath caught. She remembered the cold, the wind, the woman's trembling hands.

"I just... I didn't want you to be alone," Aria said softly.

"And I wasn't. Because of you."

More people came forward—each one sharing a moment Aria had nearly forgotten. The young mother whose child she'd helped. The man she'd comforted in the waiting room. The teenager she'd listened to when no one else would.

Small moments. Quiet kindnesses.

But to them, they were everything.

Then her mom handed her an envelope, grinning like she'd just pulled off the heist of the century.

"Mom, if this is another blind date setup, I swear—"

"It's not. It's a real vacation."

Aria opened it slowly.

Inside: tickets to The Bahamas. Ten glorious days of hammocks, ocean breeze, and exactly zero hospital alarms.

"You've been promising yourself a break for years," her mom said. "Time to cash in."

Aria stared at the tickets, her vision blurring. She wanted to say something profound, something worthy of the moment, but all that came out was a choked laugh.

"I... I don't know what to say."

"Say yes," her dad called from the grill. "And bring us back some of those little soaps."

***

That night, back in her apartment, Aria sat in The Throne with Luna purring in her lap. The bracelet caught the lamplight, the butterfly charm glinting softly.

She thought about all the letters, the gifts, the people at the cookout. She thought about how much she'd been giving without realizing she was running on empty.

But now?

Now, she was learning to receive. To let herself be seen. To accept that her kindness mattered—not just to others, but to her own healing too.

She glanced at her phone. Mrs. Wong had sent a text earlier:

*"David asks if you like Thai food. He says he knows a great place. Very romantic. Also has spring rolls."*

Aria laughed, shaking her head.

Maybe she'd take Mrs. Wong up on it. Because a man with action figures, a mom who made extra spring rolls, and a deep appreciation for Chewbacca's emotional complexity? Stranger things had happened.

She typed back:

*"Tell David I'll think about it. But only if he promises not to quiz me on the prequels."*

The response was immediate:

*"He says that is fair. He also says the prequels are controversial anyway."*

Aria smiled, setting her phone down.

In that moment, she realized healing didn't always come from grand gestures or white coats. Sometimes, it came in handwritten notes, surprise poetry, grilled hot dogs, or in the gentle purring of a cat who never judged.

She had spent so long pouring herself into others, not realizing how much she needed to be poured back into.

But now she knew.

And maybe—just maybe—she'd let herself imagine a future where she didn't have to choose between giving and receiving. Where she could be both the healer and the healed.

Sun on her skin. Coconut water in hand. Luna being pampered by her best friend back home. And who knows? Maybe even a date with a Star Wars nerd who understood that sometimes, the Force is just another word for love.

She closed her eyes, bracelet warm against her wrist, and whispered to the quiet room:

"Thank you."

And for the first time in a long time, she meant it—for others, yes, but also for herself.

Because butterflies don't ask for applause.

They just keep flying.

be enough for you
let the rest of the world tap its foot and
wait in line like everyone else

# Crosswalk Pause

I STOP AT the red light, the world halting with me. The wind is soft, barely stirring, and for a moment, the city feels muted—like someone turned the volume down. Across the street, an elderly man begins to cross. Cane tapping rhythmically. One deliberate step, then another.

He isn't hurrying. He isn't trying to.

And somehow, no one around him is either. The cars behind me stay still, like we've all agreed, without saying a word, to let this moment stretch. There's no honking. No engines revving. Just the quiet choreography of slowing down.

I watch him—his careful balance, the slight lean forward, the way he studies each step before taking it. He moves like time has bent gently around him, giving space instead of pressure. Something in me softens. My fingers loosen on the steering wheel. My breath evens out without asking.

I realize how much of my day is spent rushing through it, skipping over the in-between. But here—right now—there's nothing else to do but wait. And witness.

The light turns green. He's nearly to the curb now.

I stay still until he's safely on the sidewalk, and only then do I move forward—slower than before, like maybe I've remembered something I didn't know I'd forgotten.

# Not Her Emergency

MY PHONE LIT up in the middle of dinner.

His name.

A flurry of frantic messages, breathless with panic.

"Please. I just need five minutes. I messed up. I don't know who else to call."

There was a time I would've dropped everything—fork midair, heart racing, mind already sprinting through worst-case scenarios. I would've gone into fix-it mode without hesitation. Not because he deserved it, but because back then, I didn't know I didn't have to.

But this time, I didn't move.

Not even a twitch.

I watched the steam curl up from my plate, warm and steady. The soft clink of silverware, the quiet hum of the evening. I took another bite. Chewed slowly. Swallowed fully. And felt it—not a surge of adrenaline, but the strange, steady calm of someone who finally knows:

This is not my emergency.

Not anymore.

He used to make everything feel urgent.

Every mistake became my responsibility.

Every failure, my fault.

I was the soft place he crashed after chaos—never mind that he was the one setting fire to the ground beneath us.

And I let it happen.

For years, I mistook codependency for care.
Confused being needed with being loved.
Believed that if I could just stay steady enough, soft enough,
understanding enough, he'd eventually find his way back to sanity.
To me.
To us.

But all it ever did was leave me emptied.
Worn out.
Tethered to someone who only reached for me when the walls were
closing in.

Tonight, I didn't reach back.

Not because I don't care. I do. In the distant, quiet way you care about
someone who once held your heart with unsteady hands and dropped it
too many times to count. I don't hate him. I hope he's okay. I hope he
finds the help he needs.

But I'm not it.

I've stopped answering alarms I didn't set.
Stopped setting myself on fire to warm someone who only shows up
when he's cold.
Stopped believing that loving someone means rescuing them from their
own wreckage.

So I finished my dinner.
Washed the dishes.
Lit a candle.
Read a few pages of a book that didn't make me feel like I was too much
or not enough.

And when I crawled into bed, I felt something deeper than relief.

I felt free.

Not in a loud, defiant way. Not in a victory speech.
Just in the quiet, grounded knowing that his chaos is no longer my calling.
His storm is not my shelter to build.
His fire is not mine to put out.

He'll figure it out. Or he won't.
But either way, I'll be here.
Whole. Untouched. Unavailable.

And that's the shift.

Not a slammed door. Not a final fight.

Just a woman, calm and quiet, eating her dinner—
while the past tries to pull her back—
and she, without a word,
lets it burn.

# *Grit*

No natural gift, no easy stride,
No blazing talent born inside.
The gifted rise, the brilliant fly,
But I have something they can't buy.

I may not be extraordinarily skilled,
But I am extraordinarily willed.
This flame that burns, relentless, true,
Will push me through what others can't pursue.

I will not stop,
Not when the climb feels steep, the bottom dropped.
I will not break,
My resolve won't bend, won't shift, won't shake.
I will not fold.
This stubborn fire, fierce and bold,
Will pull me past the point of doubt—
My sheer determination will see me out.

# Eye Contact

IT HAPPENED IN line at the grocery store, somewhere between the freezer aisle and the hum of fluorescent lights. A little boy—maybe five—was perched in a cart ahead of me, legs swinging, eyes steady. He stared right at me. Not in the distracted way kids sometimes do, but directly. Quietly.

I waited for him to look away. He didn't.

So I held it. His gaze. Just to see what would happen.

And in that strange, still second, something passed between us. A kind of quiet knowing. No smile, no nod—just recognition. Like he saw me before I remembered how to be seen. Like I was there, really there, for a moment.

His mother turned and handed him a snack. He blinked, the moment gone.

But I'm still carrying it.

failure is an event
it's never a Person

# The Cracks in the Kitchen Tiles

The yelling started low, a rumbling storm,
Downstairs, where grown-ups usually kept warm.
But tonight, the kitchen tiles, once bright and clean,
Seemed to absorb the anger, sharp and mean.
Her voice, a jagged edge I'd never known,
His, a thunder that could shatter bone.
Words like glass, they flew across the room,
Leaving behind a suffocating gloom.

I huddled close, outside their slamming door,
My little brother's hand gripped tight in mine.
He's only six, he doesn't know the score,
Just that the air is thick, and feels unkind.
Then came the silence, heavier than sound,
A fragile peace that felt like breaking soon.
I saw her face, when she finally turned around,
Streaked with wetness, beneath the kitchen moon.
He packed a bag, a hollow, hollow sound,
Like something precious tumbling to the floor.
"It's for the best," were the only words he'd found,
And walked right out, and wasn't there no more.

At school, the whispers followed in the hall,
"Her mom moved out," "His dad's got someone new."
It feels like every grown-up's starting to fall,
Like houses built on sand, just breaking through.
Sarah's crying in the bathroom stall,

Her dad's on the phone, his voice all tight and low.
It's catching, this breaking, taking hold of all
The solid things we thought we used to know.

My brother asks where Daddy went to stay,
His small face crumpled, needing to believe.
I tell him stories, making hurt go away,
But inside, my own heart starts to grieve.
I check his homework, make his peanut spread,
Tuck him in tight, against the rising fear.
It feels like suddenly, inside my head,
Another grown-up, heavy, has appeared.

I miss the laughter, the easy, simple days,
Before the cracks appeared upon the wall.
Now every corner holds a hazy maze,
And I'm just trying not to let us fall.
This isn't how the stories used to go,
The happy endings, safe and warm and bright.
Now everything feels shaky, down below,
And I'm just a kid, lost in the endless night.

A year has now passed, the seasons turned anew,
The kitchen tiles still bear their silent lines.
But through the cracks, a different light shines through,
A strength I didn't know was truly mine.
My brother still asks, sometimes with a sigh,
But his small face holds more smiles now, bright and free.

We've built new stories, just him and I,
And found a rhythm in our company.
Mom's laughter echoes, though in a new space,
Her hugs feel tighter, filled with newfound grace.
We have our movie nights, a cherished place,
And her strong arms still hold me in their embrace.
Sarah's dad is better, his voice rings clear,
And in the halls, the whispers fade away.
We learned that breaking doesn't mean all fear,
But sometimes makes a brighter, stronger day.

I still miss Daddy, the way things used to be,
But life has shown a different path to roam.
And though the cracks remain for all to see,
They haven't shattered our small, growing home.

So even in the shadows, hope can bloom,
A quiet knowing, steady and so true.
We found our footing, stepping out of gloom,
And I'm not just a kid lost anymore, are you?

# The Apology Tour

IT STARTED WITH an email to my former roommate. Subject line: "Hey, sorry I disappeared during your birthday party (and the six months after)."

I hit send and immediately unplugged my router. Not sure why. Felt like something people do in movies to escape consequences.

The thing is, I wasn't trying to make amends like a hero. I wasn't writing a memoir. I was just tired of carrying around the heavy suitcase of people I used to text back. I figured if I could unzip it, maybe let a few ghosts out, I might breathe easier.

So I made a list. People I ghosted during the worst of it. Friends, almost-lovers, my dentist. I started calling it The Apology Tour, because naming it something slightly ridiculous made it easier to do.

First stop: Jason. I showed up at his bakery on a Wednesday.

"I'm sorry," I said. "For vanishing. For not answering your 'are you alive?' messages. I was alive. Just not... here."

He blinked. I braced for impact.

"Do you want a sandwich?" he asked.

That's how it went, mostly. Some people hugged me. Some didn't. One person told me, flatly, "Oh, I assumed you were dead." Another said, "I forgot about you, honestly, but this is nice."

I kept going. Each conversation like removing a pebble from my shoe. Some pebbles had been there so long I forgot I was limping.

I never apologized well. I was awkward. I fumbled. I made bad jokes. But I meant it. That counted for something, I think.

At some point, I realized I wasn't just apologizing to them. I was apologizing to myself. For disappearing. For thinking I had to hide my hurt until it wasn't ugly anymore.

The tour ended quietly—no grand finale. Just me, sitting on a park bench with a warm coffee and a sense that I'd reentered the world.

And the next time someone texted, "Hey, you good?"
I answered.

# April 27

I didn't do everything today—but I did enough.

It's almost midnight, and I'm sitting in bed with my journal balanced on my knee, the warm light from my lamp casting soft shadows across the page. The rest of the house is quiet, the kind of silence that only comes when everyone else is asleep and the pressure of the day has finally exhaled.

Today, I folded some of the laundry. Not all of it. The socks are still tangled at the bottom of the basket, the shirts still wrinkled and waiting. But the towels are folded and put away in the hallway closet. That used to be something I'd ignore or scold myself over. "Half isn't done," I'd think. But tonight, I'm choosing to see it differently.

Half is still progress. Half is more than nothing. Half means I showed up for myself in a small but real way.

I also drank more water than usual, answered that one email I'd been avoiding, and I even caught myself smiling at something stupid on TV. That counts. That definitely counts.

It wasn't a perfect day, but perfection isn't the goal anymore. Showing up, even halfway, is something. And tonight, I'm choosing to be proud of that.

So here's to small wins, quiet progress, and soft grace.

More tomorrow, maybe.
But for today, this is enough.

# The Elves in Traffic Lights

ELVES CHANGING TRAFFIC lights...
that's what childhood must feel like.

That's what she said—my sister.
Same age.
Same street.
Same car.
We were stuck in traffic, the kind that makes the air heavy and the silence louder. She was smiling, eyes distant, like she'd just remembered a secret too old to still be sweet.

I blinked. "Elves?"

She nodded. "I used to think there were little ones living inside the lights. Changing red to green. Like a job. Like magic."

And there it was—that look on my face. Not disbelief at her imagination, but a kind of awe at how I'd never once thought anything like that.

My eyebrows knit in confusion. My eyes wide, like they were trying to see her version of the world.
Can you imagine?
I couldn't.
But I tried anyway.

Because I did wonder about things like traffic lights.
I was curious too.
But instead of inventing stories, I just made mental notes.

Waited for logic to arrive—
in a book,
from someone older,
or just from watching long enough.

And in that moment,
I wondered if maybe that was what being a child was:
Believing in elves behind glass and light.

And maybe I was never really a child
in the way most people mean.

But here's the truth I almost forgot:

I did have a vivid imagination.
Not for explaining the world,
but for reshaping it.
I didn't wait for magic—
I created it.
Quietly.
With my own rules.

I might not have imagined elves,
but I imagined whole new worlds.

I'd slip myself into TV shows
and rewrite the scenes—
make them fairer,
funnier,
or just make someone finally say
what no one ever said.
In my mind, the streets could be pink if I felt silly,
trees could hang upside down
just to see how it made me feel.

No one had to wait for the answers—
because I could build a world
where the answers already existed,
tucked inside a moment I made.

It wasn't the kind of magic you could point to.
It didn't blink green or red.
But it was mine.

And still, as I stared at the traffic light that day,
red and glowing like it had something to prove,
a part of me actually squinted,
half-expecting to catch a glimpse—
just one tiny elf on his lunch break,
munching a donut,
sipping his coffee,
maybe complaining about overtime.

I didn't believe in that kind of magic.
But I admired it.

That memory didn't hurt me.
But it reminded me.
That healing isn't just about what was missing—
it's also about honoring what was always there.

And what was there,
even then,
was me.

# Please Clap (No, Seriously)

"YOU'RE NOT GOOD enough, and you never will be," said the voice in my head—rude, always choosing violence—while I stood frozen under a spotlight that felt less like stage lighting and more like the unforgiving glare of a heat lamp aimed at a particularly nervous rotisserie chicken.

There I was, center stage, feeling like every eyeball in the room had x-ray vision—because surely they could see the panic party raging inside me. My heart was playing a remix of Flight of the Bumblebee, my lungs had apparently gone on strike, and my inner monologue had become a full-blown roast session.

"Why did I agree to this?" I thought, not for the first time. I could've been home, in pajamas, binge-watching documentaries and pretending that counted as productivity. But no—I had decided to "face my fears." Classic mistake.

"They'll see right through you," that voice nagged. "You're a fraud." It had been my toxic ride-or-die since childhood, like a worst-friend-forever. I scanned the crowd for a familiar face, someone who might give me an encouraging nod or at least a thumbs-up. Instead, I saw blank expressions, one guy yawning (thanks, Chad), and a woman clearly judging my outfit.

My palms were sweaty—like, *Mom's spaghetti* levels of sweaty. My legs were halfway to becoming jelly. I couldn't tell if I was going to faint or break into an impromptu interpretive dance. Both felt equally likely.

Flashback to me at eight years old, holding up a homemade science poster titled "Do Plants Like Music?" while praying the class wouldn't laugh at my colorful chart comparing Beethoven to Britney Spears. (Spoiler: they laughed. Hard.) My tiny soul had crumbled like a stale cookie that day, and apparently, that cookie still haunted me.

But then there was my mom's voice—my real one, not the mental heckler. "You are capable of more than you know," she'd told me, gently patting my science project as if it wasn't held together by hope and glue sticks. "Believe in yourself, and others will too."

So here I was again, years later, on stage with trembling hands and a brain determined to stage a walkout. But I inhaled, exhaled (slightly wheezed), and began:
"Good evening, everyone," I said, voice just a bit wobbly. "Tonight, I want to talk about fear—and how it's been my most committed relationship."

Laughter. Sweet, glorious laughter. I wasn't sure if they were laughing with me or at me, but I didn't care. They weren't booing. That was good enough.

I told them about my essay competition heartbreak, my chronic overthinking, and my habit of dodging challenges like they were suspicious leftovers in the back of the fridge. I even admitted to skipping a friend's wedding because I was too anxious to make small talk with strangers wearing pastel.

And the more I spoke, the lighter I felt. I watched faces in the crowd soften, nods of recognition ripple through the room. Apparently, I wasn't the only one who'd lost wrestling matches with self-doubt at 3 a.m.

I said, "Confidence isn't something you find in a cereal box or win in a raffle. It's built, slowly and awkwardly, one terrifying step at a time."

I shared about volunteering to lead a work project that I was 87% sure would crash and burn. It didn't. It actually went... okay. Which, for me, was a monumental victory. I talked about going to social events alone and making it through without hiding in the bathroom the entire time.

And then I told them the truth—that this very speech was almost canceled because I had convinced myself I had nothing worth saying. But my best friend's words echoed in my mind: "You're stronger than you think. Also, I will personally drag you onstage if you back out." (She's supportive in a terrifying way.)

The room fell silent as I finished. Not a tense, awkward silence—but one that felt full. Full of connection. Of shared struggles. Of people realizing maybe they weren't as alone in their fear as they thought.

"And so," I said, "I stand here today not as a motivational guru or fearless warrior. Just as someone who's learning, one shaky step at a time, to stop letting fear drive the car. It still rides shotgun, sometimes backseat. But I've changed the playlist, and I'm the one steering."

The applause was thunderous—at least to my ears. I stepped off the stage not like a hero, but like someone who'd finally stopped apologizing for taking up space.

And that's when I realized:
Maybe I am good enough.
Maybe we all are.
Even if our science projects bomb and our inner voice is a sarcastic troll.

Because life? Life is like a garden. You don't always know what will grow. But with a little sunlight, some water, and a whole lot of awkward courage —sometimes the most unexpected flowers bloom.

# The Piano of Our Days

Before you stretches life's expanse of keys,
Where ivory gleams with promises of ease.
The white notes offer brightness, clear and loud,
Of golden hours and hearts unbowed.

But look—the black keys rise between,
A different truth, a darker scene.
They stand as sentinels of shade,
Reminders of the price we've paid,
In grief's deep well, where sorrow dwells,
A haunting tune the spirit tells.

Yet listen carefully—the beauty grows
Not from the light alone, but what it knows
Of darkness too. The black keys lend
A weight, a truth we can't pretend
Away. Without their somber tone,
The music's shallow, all alone.

So play it all, the joy, the ache,
Let every feeling find its place.
The white keys leap, the black ones mourn,
And from them both, the song is born.
Accept the shadow and the sun,
For sorrow too makes us who we've become.

# Feel What You Feel.

Emotions are messengers, not enemies.
Let yourself experience them fully,
without rushing to fix or dismiss them.
Emotional honesty opens the door to deeper healing

# The Shape of Enough

*"No one asked, but I grew anyway."* — *Anonymous Thought, Loudly Lived*

DO YOU EVER look in the mirror and see a stranger staring back at you?

I never thought I'd be that girl. You know, the one analyzing herself like a crime scene photo—zooming in on every perceived flaw like she's a detective of her own demise. But there I was, standing in front of my bathroom mirror under the worst lighting known to man, pinching at the soft parts of my stomach like they were foreign invaders.

It didn't start with a tragic moment or a dramatic breakdown. No, it started with a few harmless Instagram likes—little dopamine sprinkles. Then came the follows. Fitness influencers with abs sharp enough to slice cheese. Models with skin smoother than freshly waxed marble. Celebrities who seemed genetically engineered in a lab called "Perfection™." I fell down the rabbit hole. And unlike Alice, I didn't find wonder—just self-loathing with good lighting.

Magazines didn't offer a lifeline either. They screamed at me with headlines like, "Drop 10 Pounds in 10 Days!"—as if my body was an overdue Amazon package that needed to be returned ASAP. I started to believe that my value was inversely proportional to the number on the scale. Smaller number? Bigger worth. Simple math. Toxic math.

TV wasn't any better. It was like every channel was sponsored by "Your Body is Wrong, Fix It Inc." Reality shows, commercials, even cooking shows—because God forbid a woman just eats something without a side of guilt.

So I did what we all do when we feel like crap: I went full-in. Keto, Paleo, fasting, juice cleanses that tasted like regret blended with grass clippings. I became a calorie-counting cyborg with a gym membership and a death wish for carbs. I tracked every macro like it was national security.

And still… I didn't feel "fixed." I felt like a walking contradiction—thinner, but heavier with shame. Stronger, but weaker in spirit. It was never enough. I was never enough.

And then there was The Voice. My voice. Deep. Raspy. Unapologetically unfeminine. Like I swallowed gravel as a child and washed it down with whiskey. I used to say I sounded like Batman's sister who got into slam poetry. I didn't know a single girl who sounded like me. I felt like a lab experiment in femininity gone wrong.

And let's talk body hair. I had enough to knit a small sweater, or maybe just a stylish leg-warmer collection. I used to joke that if I ever got lost in the woods, I could braid my leg hair into a survival rope. At least I'd be the warmest corpse in any survival movie.

But oh, the irony. I worked myself to exhaustion, lost the weight, achieved the "ideal" body. I became the before-and-after pic I once worshiped. And guess what? Crickets. The compliments stopped. The same guys who once showed interest now asked, "Are you okay?" or worse, "You looked better before."

Seriously? After all that pain, sweat, and sacrifice, I was supposed to reverse it?

That's when it hit me like a protein bar to the face: Who the hell was I trying to impress? The same society that tells you to shrink, then scolds you for disappearing? The same men who fetishize curves but fear "too much confidence"? It was a losing game, and I had bought a lifetime membership.

Looking back, I realize the universe had been trying to talk some sense into me long before I was ready to listen. I remember being a kid—probably around eleven—sitting on the carpet in front of the TV, watching "Hannah Montana." There was Miley Cyrus, wig on, glitter everywhere, belting out a song with that gravelly, unmistakably deep voice. And I remember thinking, Huh. She kinda sounds like me.

But that was it. No epiphany. No emotional breakthrough. Just a passing observation from a girl too caught up in wanting to sound like a Disney princess, not like the rockstar in cowboy boots. The seed was there, but it stayed buried. I didn't know how to water it yet.

It wasn't until I heard Tracy Chapman's voice years later—rich, grounded, unapologetically deep—that something clicked. Then Maya Angelou's poetry hit me like a gospel, and I felt seen in a way I'd never allowed myself to feel before. And that's when the memory of Miley came back, like a ghost whispering, You could've known this sooner… if you'd just believed you were allowed to sound like yourself.

That was the turning point. I began detoxing—not just my body, but my feed, my mind, my life. I unfollowed every influencer who made me feel like a half-eaten sad sandwich. I ditched the magazines and started reading things that actually made me think, not shrink. I gave my TV remote the cold shoulder.

The voices in my head? Still there. Still rude. But quieter now, like they're starting to question their own authority.

And I began to embrace my quirks. My leg hair became my unsung superhero. I always knew when a bug landed on me—nature's alarm system. My deep voice? Turns out it's great for phone interviews, scaring telemarketers, and winning Halloween costume contests as Darth Vader without needing a mask.

I stopped trying to be someone else's idea of "pretty" and started reclaiming mine. Messy, hairy, raspy, sarcastic—me.

So if you're out there, staring in the mirror, wondering why you can't be "that girl," let me say this loud, deep, and clear:

You are not a problem to be fixed. You are a person to be loved.

And in case you need a laugh? Just remember: If civilization ever ends, I'll be the last woman standing, warm, hairy, and using my leg-hair rope to pull everyone to safety.

the bravest person in the room isn't the
expert—it's the one sweating through
their fear and still showing up anyway

# Cracked Mug

I FOUND IT at the back of the cupboard, tucked behind mismatched bowls and a jar of something expired. The old mug—white, chipped on one side, the handle glued back on with the kind of care that says someone couldn't quite let it go.

I don't know why I picked it up.
Maybe it was the weight of it.
Or the way it still fit in my hand, familiar without trying. Like muscle memory. Like something that had waited quietly to be remembered.

It used to be hers.

She drank tea from it every morning. Sat by the window, humming under her breath, fingers curled around the ceramic like it held more than just heat. It was a rhythm, not loud but steady—warm water, quiet chair, that mug. Her way of saying, I'm here today. Still here.

I used to think it was just a mug. Just another thing in the kitchen. But now, holding it again, I understand—it was part of her softness. Her staying power. Her gentleness, poured into daily things.

I fill it with water. Just to see if it leaks.

It doesn't.

I sit at the table. The same one we used to gather around, elbows touching, laughter layered over old placemats. Morning light filters through the curtains and lands right where she used to sit. The steam curls up from the mug like breath.

The crack along the side catches the light in a soft, silver thread.

I run my finger along it. Not to fix it—just to know it. To trace what held, even after breaking.

And somehow, I feel steadier.

Maybe we don't always need to put things back the way they were. Maybe we just need to honor what remains.

Some cracks aren't endings.
Just quiet evidence that something lived, and was loved, and mattered enough to mend.

I take a sip.
Close my eyes.
Let the warmth settle where the ache used to be.

And for the first time in a long time, the missing doesn't feel like pain.

It just feels like love—
still here, in small, ordinary things.

Still here.

# *Do. It. Anyway.*

I know it's not fair.
That you never got to taste the sky you were born to fly in.
Never touched the stage your soul rehearsed for.
Watched your dreams drift by like trains you missed—
doors closed,
windows fogged,
tracks disappearing into other people's futures.

And now,
you see them—
bright-eyed, half your age,
already conquering kingdoms you only dared to imagine.
Sculpting their lives from marble,
while you're still chiseling through doubt.

And yeah, it stings.
Because deep down you knew—
you know—what you were capable of.
But this? This is not your life to steal.

You can't wear their triumphs like a second skin.
Can't live through them like a ghost in their bones.
You'll only become the weight they trip over—
fear with your voice,
doubt with your face,
speedbumps built from your silence.

But listen...

You can live again.
Not as the shadow—
but the torch.

Be proud.
Walk with them.
Speak light into their steps where yours once faltered.
Be the hand you never had.
The voice you needed.
The open door no one held for you.

And no—
you may never get a grand thank you.
No applause,
no flowers,
no chapters with your name in bold.

But so what.
Do it anyway.

Because every time they win,
yeah—it might break you open.
Tears will fall for the life you never lived.
A soft mourning in the corner of your chest.

But so what.

Do. It. Anyway.

Healing doesn't always roar.
Sometimes, it's just the sound of your own
voice
whispering through the crack in the
mirror

—


I'm still here.
And I'm not done yet.

your hand on my back—
no words needed to unbreak
what the world shattered

# The Crying Bench

IT WASN'T OFFICIAL or anything, but that bench was mine.

Every Tuesday, same spot in the park, under the tree that looked like it had regrets. I'd sit, pretend I was just out getting fresh air, and cry behind my sunglasses. Quietly. Politely. The way you're supposed to.

It started after everything fell apart. You know the kind of fall where even gravity seems surprised. I didn't want people asking if I was okay. I didn't want anyone to tell me it would get better. I just wanted that bench. That hour. Those tears.

Then one Tuesday, someone was already there.

A man. Older. Rumpled coat. He wasn't crying, exactly. But he looked like he had been. Or was about to. We didn't speak. He just scooted over a bit, left room like maybe he recognized the grief posture. I sat. We stared ahead like two sad pigeons.

Next week, he was gone. But there was a note under the bench.

Folded in half. On notebook paper. No envelope. It said:
"Crying Bench, huh? Guess we've both got great taste in places to fall apart."

I snorted. Out loud. Which felt like breaking a rule.

The week after, I left one back:
"Better than crying in line at the DMV. Barely."

That was how it started.

We never signed our names. Just left notes, folded and tucked under the bench like little grief time capsules. Some were funny:
"Today I cried so hard I scared a squirrel."
Some were strange:
"Do you think trees notice when we're sad under them?"
Some cracked something open:
"He died on a Tuesday. I hate how Tuesdays keep coming anyway."

We never ran into each other again, not really. I saw him once across the park, walking away. He had a note in his hand.

Weeks passed. The notes got longer. Messier. One said:
"My daughter used to call me a walking hug. Now I feel like a hollow shell in a coat."

I replied:
"Maybe we're still walking hugs. Just more of a slow shuffle now."

Healing didn't come in some grand epiphany. No lightning. No montage. Just a slow, awkward stumble. Like wearing borrowed shoes that don't quite fit—you can walk, but you're aware of every step.

But I started crying less. And when I did, it wasn't the heavy kind that drags your ribs down with it. More like a leak. Manageable.

One day, I left a note that said:
"I smiled yesterday. It felt weird. But I didn't hate it."

His last note, weeks later, just said:
"I think I'm ready to sit on other benches now. Thank you."

I stayed a little longer that day. Ran my hand along the worn wood of the bench. Watched a squirrel do something deeply chaotic with a Cheeto. I didn't cry.

I just sat there, grateful that two strangers had decided to fall apart in the same place—and somehow, started to put each other back together.

Quietly. Politely. The way healing sometimes is.

# The Truest Yes

Within you stirs a quiet call,
A dream that echoes through it all.
You search the faces gathered near,
Hoping someone else might hear.

But wait—and let this truth sink in:
The blueprint living deep within
Was drawn for you alone to trace,
A flame no other soul can place.

So move forward, brave and free,
Write the tale you're meant to be.
Though others cannot see it yet,
This fire you hold—don't you forget—

Belongs to you, and you alone,
A seed that's yours to make full-grown.
The nods you seek will come and go,
But you're the only yes
you'll ever need to know.

# Rooms Without Answers

IT STARTED WITH the sound of her breath—shallow, a little uneven. I could tell she'd been crying before I came in. I didn't ask. I just slipped under the blanket beside her, the old one with fraying edges we used to make forts with when the world was less complicated.

We lay there at an odd angle with our heads almost touching, staring at the ceiling like it held secrets. She didn't speak for a long time, and I didn't rush her. There was a rhythm to the silence, like waves pulling us into the same emotional current. Then, quietly, almost like she was afraid the words might break something:

"I don't know how to be okay," she said.

I felt my chest tighten in that old familiar way—the kind of ache that never really leaves, just settles in your ribs and waits for moments like this to stir.

I wanted to tell her everything I'd learned. About years of therapy, about numbness masquerading as strength, about how sometimes healing looks like making your bed or saying no or crying over toast. But it felt like too much. Like handing someone a novel when all they can carry is a page.

Instead, a tear slipped down the side of my face and I whispered, "I can't help you with your emotions, but I can support you enough to give you relief and space for healing."

She didn't say anything right away. Her pinky nudged mine. That was enough.

Because maybe that's the most honest kind of love—not solving, not saving, just staying. Quietly. Gently. Knowing where you end and they begin, and loving them enough to let them do the work, but never alone.

And for the first time in a long time, I didn't feel guilty for not having all the answers.

Just tired.

But also—light.

every scar tells a story i survived
every tear was a lesson keeping me alive
the silence inside me
is starting to sing
a fragile beginning
but hope takes wing
i am rising
not just surviving
finding strength
in the cracks of my soul
i am healing
slowly breathing
turning pain
into power i own


*broken pieces can still find peace.*

# The Shoes Don't Fit Anymore

I FOUND THEM in the back of the closet. Dusty. Curled at the toes. Faded just enough to feel like memory. Old sneakers I used to wear every day, back when I didn't think much about where I was going—only how fast I could get there.

On impulse, I sat down on the edge of the bed that once belonged to a much smaller version of me and tried them on.

They didn't fit.
Not even close.
My heel wouldn't slide in. My toes curled uncomfortably against the worn fabric. It was ridiculous—how genuinely surprised I was. As if I'd expected my body to pause in time, waiting for me to catch up.

I took them off and just held them for a while.
Something about them felt heavier than shoes should be.

They reminded me of a person I kept trying to be.
The good kid. The easy one. The version that never questioned, never strayed too far from the path laid out for them. The one who wore those shoes like armor, running hard and fast toward a life someone else dreamed for me.

I carried so much guilt for growing past that version.
For not staying small.
For wanting things that didn't fit neatly inside the rules of this house.
I thought I owed it to everyone to keep wearing that identity—tight, uncomfortable, blistering—but familiar.

But sitting there with those too-small shoes in my hands, it hit me.
They were never meant to grow with me.
They served their time.
Carried me through scraped knees and long walks home and all the quiet
pretending I didn't have questions I wasn't allowed to ask.

And now?
Now, they don't fit. And that's not a betrayal—it's a sign.
A quiet one, but clear.

You don't shrink to fit the past.
You thank it for getting you this far, and then you put it down gently.

I placed the shoes back in the closet. Not out of shame. Not with grief.
But with something that felt a little like grace.

Because for the first time in years, I didn't feel guilty for becoming
someone else.
Someone larger.
Wider in spirit.
Louder in truth.
More fully formed.

And I walked out of that room barefoot,
but not lost.
Not searching.
Just free.

**Some shoes aren't meant to last forever.**
**Some selves aren't either.**

# The Voice Memo

I'D FORGOTTEN ABOUT it until today. The voicemail. The one I definitely shouldn't have left. The one I recorded in a manic fit of desperation, probably around 2 a.m., three cocktails deep and armed with a complete lack of self-respect.

But today, I found it. Buried in my old voice memos, underneath a shopping list that reads "milk, sanity, more wine." And yes, I hit play. Why? Because I hate myself. But also—curiosity. Like how people slow down when they drive by a car wreck.

The first thing I hear is my voice, slurring just enough to make me sound like I've been living in a bar for three years. "Heyyy," I begin, and I immediately regret it. "I... I just need to talk to you. About us. About what we were... okay, what you did, but also—what I didn't do—"

I stop it. I stop it hard, because the cringe is already making my skin crawl, but, no, I need to finish this. So, I hit play again. The trainwreck needs to be seen.

My voice crackles in with more liquid confidence. "I don't even know what I'm asking for. Maybe an apology, maybe closure, maybe you to get yourself together, but whatever it is, I—" I pause, and then I swear to God, I cry. Like, full sobs. "Why do you never answer my calls?"

I have to laugh. It's a harsh, wheezy sound that feels like a real, legitimate panic attack mixed with a bad case of secondhand embarrassment. This was me?

I press play again, against my better judgment, and I hear myself beg, "I just want to know that you care, you know? Like, I can't—don't leave me like this. I can't do this alone, please."

Oh my God, I sound like a dying puppy. I sound pathetic. If I were my ex, I would've blocked me immediately after the first "hey."

But the real kicker comes about 30 seconds later. I sound like I'm making a dramatic point and then, without warning, I hiccup, loudly. "I... I can't... I—hic—can't believe—hic—this is happening."

I hit pause and set my phone down. I laugh again, louder this time, even though I'm alone. Because that version of me? That drunken, desperate, I-might-need-a-therapist version? It sounds so completely foreign. Who was she? She's like a ghost—pathetic, emotional, clinging to someone who didn't deserve her.

I can't believe that was me. It's almost funny how far I've come since then. Almost.

But not that far. The voice memo ends with me saying, "Okay, well, I'll just... let you call me back whenever. Whenever you're ready. Love you."

I delete it. Instantly. Like a proper adult.

Then I laugh some more, because... love you? Really? Like we're some kind of rom-com? Jesus.

Somewhere, deep inside, I'm kind of proud of that girl. The girl who thought she needed validation from an ex who couldn't even spell "empathy." But mostly, I'm relieved I never have to hear her voice again.

And for the record? If that was me reaching for closure, I'm definitely done reaching. That's a reach I'll never make again.

# The Better What If

What if it doesn't all go to hell?

What if—just once—it's not a hard sell?

What if the path,
though cracked, though cruel,
still walks you home...
still gives you room to feel whole?

What if the risk
—the one that ties your guts in knots—
is the exact damn thing
you need to become more
than just surviving?

What if the leap
you've been circling around
is the one thing
that finally gets you off the ground?

What if the voice that says
"you'll fail,"
"you're not enough,"
"don't even try"—
isn't truth?
Just fear...
in a mask made of scars.

We all know those what ifs.
We rehearse 'em like gospel:

What if I fall?
What if I freeze?
What if I break
and nobody sees?

What if I give it everything—
and still lose?

But what if you don't?

What if you rise?

What if there's fire
you forgot inside your eyes?

What if the heartbreak,
the wreckage,
the dirt—
is the reason
you'll earn
your worth?

What if they stay?
What if they cheer?
What if you speak...
and someone actually hears?

What if the ones
who walked away
were just too small
for what you'd become someday?

What if the tears you buried deep
were feeding roots
you didn't know would ever grow?

What if the storm inside your chest
is the thing
that proves
you're blessed?

What if you're not
too messy to love?

What if you are
what you've been dreaming of?

What if that thing
that haunts your night
becomes the spark
that sets you right?

So when doubt
comes dressed like truth—

When fear
starts barking through your roof—

You don't bow.
You don't hide.

You look it dead in the eyes—
and say:

"What if GOOD still lives in me?"

Because the game we always play—
The cruel "what ifs" we spin each day—
Can break us down or build us whole.
Which game of "what if"
we choose to play
Can shape the truth of everyday.

So play it bold.
Play it raw.
Play it true.

Because what if...
the best
was always meant
for you?

# The Last Apology

I DIDN'T PLAN to write it.

It just came one night, slow and steady, like rain on a window you didn't expect. The words had been sitting somewhere deep for years—tangled up with guilt, softened by time, still sharp at the edges.

I'm sorry for how I left.
I'm sorry I made you doubt your worth just because I couldn't hold my own. I'm sorry I didn't say goodbye like you deserved.

It spilled out in a kind of silence that only comes when no one's watching.
No performance. No edits. No hope of redemption—just truth.
Raw and trembling, but finally honest.

I wrote it all.
Every fractured memory.
Every thing I wish I'd said before I burned the bridge.
I wrote until the shame loosened its grip and the ache inside my chest settled into something still.

And when I finished, I sat with it.
Read it aloud.
Felt every syllable land in my body like something sacred.

Then I folded it.
Neatly. Carefully.
Held it in my hands for a moment like it was something holy.

And I knew—I wouldn't send it.

Because it wasn't for them anymore.

It was for the version of me that wasn't forgiven.
The one who replayed that goodbye over and over, hoping to rewrite the ending. The one who stayed small beneath the weight of my own regret.

But the apology had already done its work.
It had pulled the guilt out like a splinter.
Not to forget, not to erase, but to acknowledge.
To say: I hurt someone I cared about. I wish I hadn't. But I did. And I've grown.

That was enough.

I tucked the letter away in a drawer I rarely open.
Not hidden, just resting.
A reminder that healing doesn't always look like reconciliation.
That sometimes, grace is private.
And that growth can bloom quietly, without needing to be witnessed.

That was the last apology I'll ever write them.
Not because they don't deserve it,
but because I finally understand—

**some healing is meant to stay in your own hands.**

# Look for the Good, Even in Small Things.

Gratitude shifts your focus from what's missing
to what's meaningful.
Start or end your day naming three things you're thankful for—
consistency builds resilience.

# Ashes in the Light

I USED TO think we were perfect enough, my family. Not flawless, not fairy-tale—but stitched together with enough love and laughter to hold the walls upright.

My mother, tender and wild in turns, was still learning how to be a person. Raised in the wreckage of her own childhood, she mothered five children and then tried to reclaim the girlhood she'd never had—sometimes at the wrong moments.

Okay, to be fair, it wasn't quite mothering—not in the traditional, casserole-and-bedtime-stories sense. Her version of "nurturing" mostly involved us raising each other while she reapplied her eyeliner and chased whichever man was flashing the most cash and attention that week.

Today, we'd call it neglect. Back then, we just called it Tuesday. It was chaotic, occasionally glittery, and weirdly educational—like a crash course in emotional self-sufficiency, taught by someone who never graduated herself.

My father, not by blood but by name, came into our lives quietly, but I met him with a coldness I couldn't explain. Something in me resisted him from the start. Years passed before I learned to call that resistance by gentler names: fear, grief, maybe even loyalty to what came before. Eventually, I let him in.

My older sister and I were opposites in motion—fire and shadow, always clashing. Growing up we could never seem to find the same rhythm, like two songs playing in different keys.

And then the younger girls—soft, bright things, never much for school but full of colors the world hadn't yet named. I helped raise them, tucked them in, combed out the tangles. They were the part of me I could protect.

We were messy. Wounded in different ways but we filled the kitchen with warmth, joked through dinner, shared small kindnesses that felt like proof we were okay. Maybe even whole. And for a while, I believed it. Even as the cracks began to spread, hairline and quiet, just beneath the surface of my mind.

I wasn't the oldest, just the one who grew up first. The protector. The fixer. Everyone had a place. Everyone played a role. And I played mine so well, I didn't notice the floor shifting beneath us until it gave way.

It didn't happen all at once. The unraveling came slowly, like fog rolling in —soft, but suffocating. I remember the first time I felt it: sunlight on my skin, the air thick with the smell of summer rain. But underneath that brightness, there was something else. A shadow. A coldness creeping into the corners of our home, into the quiet spaces where trust used to live.

It came in pieces—stolen glances, fragmented conversations, stories that didn't line up. Tiny betrayals, brushing against each other like dry leaves, until they caught fire and revealed something I wasn't ready to see.

My sisters. My father. My mother. Each with their own hidden wounds, their own unspoken truths tucked beneath the routines of family life. It was in the silence between us, the way we pretended not to notice, that I realized: the love I thought we had was wrapped in denial. And that denial had teeth.

I wanted to fix it. God, I wanted to fix it. I wanted to drag the truth into the light, to wash it clean, to hold each of them in my arms and press them back into something whole. I wanted to go back—before the knowing. Before the silence turned heavy. Before I realized the foundation we stood on had been cracked for years.

But the more I tried to hold it together, the more I unraveled.

Piece by piece, I crumbled under the weight of their brokenness. Their pain became my own, until I couldn't tell where theirs ended and mine began. I was vanishing—bit by bit—trying to keep them from falling apart.

And then, one night, in the quiet of my room, I let go.

I looked at my reflection—eyes dim, shoulders bowed under invisible burdens—and the truth slipped out in a whisper.

I can't fix it.

The words landed with a thud in my chest. A release that shattered something and healed it all at once. The tears came—not from anger, but from the softness of surrender. My hands trembled, reaching for nothing. And for the first time, I let them fall.

There, in the stillness, something shifted. The truth settled deep.

This was never mine to carry.

There was grace in that. Grace I didn't fully understand, but could almost feel. Like breath after drowning. Like light through a cracked window.

So I spoke again—barely a whisper, but steady.

There is Someone who knows how to make it whole.

And I leaned into that. That fragile, sacred hope. The hands that formed galaxies and traced rivers into the earth. The hands that painted skies with light and shaped bones in the womb. The hands that held grief without flinching—the hands that made us—would know what to do with all of this.

My hands were only ever meant to reach so far. But His hands… His hands can heal what I cannot.

So I wait.

Not passively, but patiently. I live in the in-between, in the hope that one day, He'll turn the ruins into something beautiful. Maybe not the way I imagined. Maybe not even in this lifetime. But in a way only He can.

Until then, I let it be. The weight is lighter now—not because I fixed anything.

But because I finally stopped trying to carry the world.

# Folded Laundry

SHE'S SITTING ON the edge of her bed, folding socks. The afternoon light makes lines on the carpet, dust floating in the still air. There's a mug on her nightstand, half-drunk tea gone cold, and the TV murmurs something low in the background—just enough to fill the space.

I'm leaning in her doorway, not sure why I came in. Just watching.

She folds with the kind of care you don't notice until you're looking for it. Each pair of socks matched, smoothed, tucked into itself like a small act of order against everything else.

She looks tired. Not just in the way she always says she is, but underneath that. Something softer. Like the kind of tired that lives in the bones. Her face is bare—no makeup, no smile—and I see the tiny lines near her mouth, the way her shoulders slope when she thinks no one's paying attention.

There's a photo on the dresser. One I've seen a hundred times but never really looked at. She's younger in it. Laughing. Her head tilted back, hair wild around her face. She looks like someone I don't know. Like someone I'd want to know.

And it hits me—quiet but hard.

She wasn't always my mom.

She had a life before I showed up and made her tired. She had dreams that weren't laundry and dinner and rides to school. She made mistakes. Got her heart broken. Had favorite songs and fears and maybe even secrets she never told anyone.

She's a person.

Not just mine.

Someone's daughter. Someone's best friend. Someone who probably still doesn't have it all figured out.

She notices me watching and raises an eyebrow. "What?" she says, a smile just barely tugging at the corner of her mouth.

"Nothing," I say. "Just… thinking."

I step into the room and sit beside her on the bed. She hands me a sock without a word.

We fold the rest together.

Quiet. Easy.

Like maybe we're both learning something.

if it's pitch black
and you can't find the light... surprise!...
it might be you

# When The Song Knows

IT STARTS WITH the opening chords—just a few notes and my stomach drops like I missed a step on the stairs. Shuffle. Always shuffle. It's supposed to keep me safe from this exact kind of emotional ambush.

But no. The universe, with its deeply questionable sense of humor, has chosen violence. And now that song is playing. The one that reminds me of him. The one we once slow-danced to in the kitchen, socks sliding on linoleum, pasta boiling over on the stove.

I should skip it. I even reach for the button.

Instead, I let it play.

The lyrics hit like a drunk friend telling me what I already know but don't want to hear.
"You gave it all, and he still left?"
Yes, Brenda, thank you for that poetic gut punch.

I'm in the car, parked outside the grocery store. I haven't gone in yet. I tell myself I'm mentally preparing for spinach, but really, I'm letting a ballad from 2012 absolutely wreck me in the Safeway parking lot.

I laugh a little—because it's pathetic. Then I cry a little—because it's still true.

A man walks past with a cart full of orange soda and cat litter. He gives me the quick glance people give women crying in cars: a mix of concern and "not my circus."

Fair.

But I let the song keep playing. All the way through. No fast-forwarding, no hiding. I even hum along at the end—quietly, out of tune, but still. A small, defiant act of survival.

When it's over, I take a breath. My face is blotchy. My heart feels like it's been through a spin cycle. But weirdly, I feel lighter. Like maybe something got sung out of me.

I wipe my eyes with the sleeve of a hoodie I haven't washed in a week. Pull the grocery list out of the passenger seat.

Spinach. Dish soap. A new playlist.

No more shuffle.

# *When I Laugh*

There's something strange about being the one who always lifts the room while quietly trying to climb out of your own pit. But it works. Laughter changes the chemistry of a room—and sometimes, if you're lucky, it changes the chemistry of your own mind.

It's not that I'm always happy. God, no. Some days the weight is so dense I feel like I'm breathing concrete.
But if I can laugh, I can breathe. And if I can breathe,
I can keep going.

Because when I laugh...
I don't remember that my father disappeared
when I was three.
Got married, lived a completely different life
in a new country
And then eight years later said
he was always looking for me.

*When I laugh...*
I don't remember that my mother sold her principles
for comfort
And stayed with her husband like his shy smile
and roving hands
Never twisted and destroyed the meaning of childhood.

*When I laugh,*
I'm thankful for the independent person that I am
I don't remember my mother's neglect
That I learned to do things like tell time based on how long it took
Bambi's mother to die.
That I have an excellent memory
Because my days were spent watching the same four tapes
Until the reels wept static—
Each time finding something new to appreciate
Babysat by cartoons that taught me how to count
and say my ABCs
Before anyone thought to enroll me in school.

*When I laugh,*
I forget the hurt I felt at five—being told to my face
by my grandmother
That I'm not her son's child,
The fact that she could account
for her son's wanderings is just wild.

*When I laugh...*
I forget that my sister stole both of my first boyfriends
Okay maybe not stole because you can't steal people
they have to go willingly
But that's what it feels like at 14
when the person you took care of though older
and gave the best portions to,
Couldn't let you have just one thing for yourself
As if betrayal was a compliment
I didn't know how to receive.

*When I laugh...*
I'm not the vending machine of comfort everyone shakes
When they want a pick-me-up,
Then walks away from once they've had their fill.

*When I laugh,*
I forget the guilt I felt—and sometimes still feel—
For deciding not to burn the world down
To avenge my little sister
Like I always promised myself I would.

*When I laugh,*
It feels normal being the strong one—
The one who never needs support, never gets a compliment.
Because it's expected.
While my sister made one phone call to Dad
And got a new engine,
Even though she ran the car dry with the check engine light on for
months.

*When I laugh,*
I forget that I ask myself almost daily "What is my life?" and "How is
this my life?" then feel guilt for seeming ungrateful for all of the
many blessings I've received inspite of the hardships and in the
midst of the storms.

*When I laugh,*
My favorite color is blue and jeans are still
for every occasion, even sleeping

not because I always wanted to be a boy
or because boys are stronger
and jeans are safer than skirts.

*When I laugh,*
For a few precious moments your pains aren't barging into my
personal space
Fighting with my pains for first place
I'm not wearing your sorrows like a second skin.

*When I laugh,*
I still believe I have broader shoulders than Atlas,
Capable of carrying and fixing everyone else.

*When I laugh,*
It's easier to forgive people who only remember me when they're
lonely,
Easier to pretend I'm not exhausted from being "resilient."

I learned to be funny
like other kids learned to ride a bike—
With scraped knees and no one holding the seat.
I fell, I bled, I got back up—
And turned it into a punchline.

Humor is mine.
No one gets to take it.
No one gets to twist it.
It's my rebellion.
My rescue.

My oxygen when the world refuses to give me air.

*When I laugh...*
I am not broken.
I am whole.
Not in spite of everything—
But because I still can.
I am just... breathing.

Humor is how I rewire the darkness.
How I talk back to the thoughts that try to convince me
I'm not enough, or too much, or broken beyond repair.

Now don't get me wrong...
When I laugh,
It's not because I'm pretending.
My smile and my laugh are not masks.
They are genuine.
*They are not denials.*
**They are defiance.**
It's because I remember who I am
without the weight.
The laughter is mine. The joy is mine.
And I choose to give the best of me—
Not because the world has earned it,
But because I have.

Not because life's been kind,
But because it hasn't—
And I'm still here.

Laughing.

**Alive.**

***And sane...***
because I choose to be.

scar under the skin—
pain that once roared now whispers
I survived this too

# Not Too Much

THERE'S A PARTICULAR kind of grief that comes from wanting water from a stone. You stand there, parched, reasonable in your thirst, watching your own need bounce off granite. And somehow—this is the cruelest part—you begin to believe the problem is the size of your thirst, not the nature of the stone.

You're not asking too much. You're just asking the wrong person.

How many years do we spend trying to grow fruit from concrete? We blame the season, adjust the soil, speak more gently to the ground. We water and wait, water and wait, convinced that our technique is flawed, our timing off, our love insufficient. Never once do we consider that some foundations were never meant to yield.

The parent who cannot see you. The friend who cannot hold you. The lover who cannot meet you. They are not broken, necessarily, and neither are you. But the math doesn't work. You are fluent in a language they have never learned, and you keep speaking, slower and louder, as if volume could translate, as if wanting could be enough.

It isn't enough. Wanting is never enough.

There's a certain violence in the way we shrink ourselves to fit into spaces that were never meant for us. We fold our needs like origami, creasing and decreasing until they're small enough, quiet enough, easy enough. We perform minimalism with our hearts. *See how little I require? See how I can survive on crumbs?* And still—still—the crumbs don't come. Or they come irregularly, unpredictably, and we call this love because we've forgotten what nourishment feels like.

You learn to apologize for needing. You learn to call yourself needy, as if need itself were shameful, as if you invented loneliness and hunger in your own image. You weren't born knowing this self-contempt. Someone taught you, wordlessly, that your requirements were too expensive, your emotional mathematics too complicated. So you tried to become simple. Tried to want less. Tried to be the kind of person who could thrive in drought.

But some of us are built for rain.

The truth—the one that sits in your throat like a stone you can neither swallow nor speak—is that you have been directing your questions to an empty room, expecting echoes to sound like answers. You have been knocking on a door that was never meant to open, not for you, not for anyone. And the failure here is not yours.

This is not about lowering your standards or raising your voice. This is not about self-improvement or self-help or ten steps to better communication. This is about recognition. This is about seeing, finally, that you've been trying to teach calculus to someone who never learned addition, and blaming yourself for their confusion.

The wrong person will make you feel like an imposition. The right person will make you feel like an inevitability.

There are people in this world who speak your language. Who won't need subtitles for your silence or footnotes for your fear. Who will meet your needs not as burdens to be carried, but as invitations to be answered. You won't have to diminish yourself to fit through their door. The door will be wide enough for all of you—the messy parts, the tender parts, the parts that need and need and need.

But first, you have to stop waiting at the wrong door.

First, you have to let yourself believe that your thirst is not evidence of your brokenness, but of your aliveness. That wanting connection, tenderness, presence, reciprocity—these are not character flaws. These are the requirements of being human. You are not too much. You have never been too much. You've just been directing your muchness toward people who only traffic in scarcity.

What if you took all that love you've been spending on convincing someone to care and spent it on finding someone who already does? What if you stopped auditioning for a role that was cast before you arrived? What if you walked away from the stone and went looking for the well?

This is not about giving up on people. This is about giving up on the fantasy that you can want something enough for both of you. That your love can be large enough to compensate for someone else's absence. It can't. It was never meant to.

You're not asking too much. You're just asking the wrong person.

And somewhere—I promise you this—somewhere there's a right person who's been looking for someone exactly like you. Someone who speaks your language fluently. Someone who won't make you feel like a burden for having needs, who won't require you to shrink or hide or apologize for taking up space. Someone who will say yes to your questions before you finish asking them, because the answer was always yes, it was just waiting for you to arrive.

But you can't meet them while you're still standing at the wrong door.

So walk away. Forgive yourself for how long you stayed, for how much you gave, for believing you could make someone ready who wasn't. Forgive yourself for not knowing what you know now. And then—this is the important part—then go find your people. The ones who make you feel possible instead of impossible. The ones who make loving you look easy, because for them, it is.

You're not asking too much.

You never were.

# Half of a Hug

THE SERVICE IS over. People are shuffling out, murmuring soft condolences like they're afraid of waking the dead. I stand by the door, coat still unbuttoned, fingers fiddling with the seam of my pocket. The air tastes like lilies and old carpet.

I don't look for him, but I know he'll come.

When he does, it's like seeing a ghost that remembers you too well. Same jawline, same eyes—older now, but still him. My brother.

We haven't spoken in seven years. Not since the last fight, the one that left us stranded on opposite sides of a silence neither of us knew how to cross.

He steps toward me. Slow. Like he's approaching something delicate. Maybe dangerous.

Then, he opens his arms. It's tentative, unsure. A peace offering made of muscle memory.

And I—I hesitate. Just for a second. My throat closes. My weight shifts back onto my heels even as my hands lift.

Then I step in, but not all the way. My arms wrap around him loosely, more out of reflex than intention. His hand rests between my shoulder blades. Mine hovers, not quite landing. My feet stay planted where they are, holding distance my arms won't.

137

It's awkward. Off-balance. Half of a hug.

But something passes between us in that crooked embrace. Heat, and breath, and the faint press of old blood still binding us underneath all the anger.

It isn't forgiveness. Not fully. But something in me loosens. Like a window cracked open in a long-locked room.

He pulls back first. His jaw works like he's swallowing words. Our eyes meet, and for a moment, we don't look away.

Then he nods—barely—and turns toward the parking lot.

I watch him go, coat still unbuttoned, hand still in my pocket.

# *Begin Again, even at the End*

The final curtain fell like stone,
Heavy velvet drawn across the light.
The script was finished, every word now flown
Into the vast and empty night.
My bones remember stories never told—
Of battles lost, of loves that slipped away.
This landscape of my life, grown bare and cold,
Offers no solace at the close of day.

Begin again?

The words sound like a curse,
A cruel demand on limbs that ache for rest.
Behind me lies a lifetime—every verse
Written in scars across my chest.

Yet still my heart, worn thin and barely whole,
Keeps beating out its stubborn, fragile song.
A whisper rises from some buried soul:
"You've sung this dirge of ending far too long."

The past clings tight like shadows in the room—
Lost laughter, broken vows, the dreams undone.
To sweep them out and let in something new
Feels heavier than all I've overcome.

But in the silence where the darkness sits,
Something small begins to wake and grow.
A seed of hope that breaks through all of this,
A quiet voice that tells me: you still know
How to refuse the surrender drawing near.
How to gather up the shattered, scattered parts,
And make a mosaic, fragile but sincere—
A different pattern than where this one starts.

Begin again,
though dusk has claimed the sky,
And every instinct begs me just to stop.
Perhaps there's strength in choosing not to die,
In planting seeds when others let them drop.

The end, it seems, a line I can't uncross—
But even at the edge, there's room to stand.
To write one chapter more despite the loss,
To whisper softly with an trembling hand:

"Though time has worn me down to bone and breath,
I choose to live, to let the morning come.
Begin again—not in defiance of death,
But because I'm still here. Still someone.
Begin again, with all that I've become.
Begin again, even at the end."

# Things That Are Still True Even on Bad Days (Yes, Even Today)

- You've made it through every disaster your brain swore would end you.

- You still deserve love, snacks, and Wi-Fi—preferably all at once.

- Your vibe is not ruined just because you wore pajama pants until 4 p.m.

- The group chat would notice if you vanished. They would also send memes to lure you back.

- That one time you said something awkward in 2017? Literally no one remembers.

- Being emotionally unstable does not cancel out how funny you are.

- Coffee still exists. So do naps. Coincidence? I think not.

- Healing is not a race, it's a chaotic relay where everyone drops the baton at least once.

- You are not too much. You're just... deeply seasoned.

- You're doing better than you think. No refunds, no take-backs, just vibes.

# His Playlist

THE DRIVE WAS quiet at first. Just the hum of the tires and the click of the turn signal. We hadn't spoken much in the waiting room. Even less in the weeks leading up to it. Too many years between us. Too many words that didn't land right.

He shifted in the seat, cleared his throat like he wanted to say something, then didn't. Just reached for the glove box, pulled out his old phone—cracked at the corners, held together by a case I gave him years ago.

"Still works," he said, almost to himself.

He connected it to the car.
Scrolled a bit.
Tapped the screen.

And suddenly we were back—
not in this car, not in this year—
but in the one from that road trip to the lake,
when I was fourteen and too proud to admit I liked the same music he did. Songs that played with the windows down and our elbows hanging out, singing off-key like it was something holy.

The first few chords came on, and my chest tightened.
I glanced at him, but he was looking straight ahead, his fingers tapping the wheel like they remembered.

And then—
right at the chorus—
we both started singing.
At the exact same time.
Same words. Same pitch. Like no time had passed at all.

And for a moment,
just a moment,
I wasn't holding the silence or the history or the weight of everything
unsaid.

I was just a son,
sitting beside his dad,
singing a song they both knew by heart.

He didn't look at me.
Didn't have to.
His voice cracked a little on the high note.
Mine did too.

Not a fix.
Not a full return.
But a thread—soft and small—pulled taut between us again.

And as the next song came on,
and we both let it play,
I realized—

Maybe not everything is lost.
Maybe some things stay quietly waiting,
right where you left them.

worthy isn't a feeling
it's a fact
(like gravity, but more flattering)

# The Right Word

THE WORD GETS stuck halfway out of my mouth.

"Um," I say, blinking too fast, "I presume…?"

Silence, just for a beat. Not sharp. Just…waiting. My pulse taps loud against the inside of my wrist.

Presume.

Is that right? Or was it assume? I've looked them up a hundred times, written their meanings in the corners of notebooks, made up silly memory tricks. But when I'm actually speaking—really speaking—I can never remember which is which.

My mouth always moves half a second ahead of my brain, and I hate it. Every sentence feels like a risk. Like I'm stepping out onto a frozen pond, waiting to hear the crack.

Nobody corrects me. Someone nods. The conversation drifts forward.

But my face burns anyway. I don't think anyone noticed, but still—I noticed. I always do.

I carry this quiet doubting around with me like an old scarf—soft, familiar, impossible to take off. I second-guess everything I say. Every meeting, every email, every "good morning." Did I sound too unsure? Too cold? Too much?

145

Even ordering coffee is a small act of bravery. I still hesitate before saying caramel, because I'm not sure if I say it weird. I probably do.

The meeting ends. People leave. I stay back, organizing my notes slower than I need to. I'm halfway to the door when he stops me—my manager. He's holding his tablet in one hand, tapping it absentmindedly with the other.

"I liked how you phrased that earlier," he says. "Presume. It was the right tone."

It takes me a second to answer. "Oh," I say. "Thanks."

He smiles and keeps walking. That's it. No applause. No spotlight.

But my chest feels a little fuller. Lighter, somehow.

Because today, the word was right.
And—maybe—so was I.

# Beyond the Green

The green-eyed serpent coiled and hissed,
Not just "I want," but "Yours I'd missed."
A shadowed wish, a twisted plea,
That joy in them should cease to be.

Then clarity, a piercing light,
This hunger born of bitter spite.
To crave and yet deny their share?
Hate masked in longing, stark and bare.

I break the chains, release the sting,
Let admiration's chorus sing.
Their light shines bright, it dims not mine,
A heart unbound, can truly shine.

NOTE: We've been taught envy is just wanting what someone else has—
but that's only the surface. It's human to desire what you admire in others.
The real danger begins when someone else's joy makes you feel worse about
your own life, or when you secretly wish they didn't have what you want—
even if you can't have it either. That's not just envy; that's resentment in
disguise—the deepest form of hatred. True healing starts when we can want
something without resenting the person who has it. Their light doesn't dim
yours.

# Backyard Fence

HE WAS HAMMERING in a new board when I showed up.
Didn't look surprised to see me.
Just nodded toward the far end of the fence and said,

"That one's loose too."

No "how've you been,"
no "I'm glad you're here."
But that was his way—never one for doorways, always halfway through
something when you arrived.

I walked over, grabbed the bucket of nails, and crouched down.
We worked like that—quiet, side by side.
The way we used to build things.
The way we used to talk without talking.

The air smelled like sun-warmed cedar and freshly cut grass.
Wind chimes knocked together in the distance, soft and accidental.
A dog barked somewhere down the street.

At some point he said,
"This thing's been falling apart for years."
I didn't ask if he meant the fence.

I looked over at him—really looked.
His hair thinner, face weathered in ways I hadn't let myself notice until
now. Hands still strong, but slower. Not shaky, just... thoughtful.
Like every movement had to earn its place.

"I didn't know if you'd come," he said.

"I wasn't sure I would."

He nodded again, like that was fair.
And it was.

We went back to hammering. Nail by nail. Panel by panel. The rhythm
filled the space between us. Not uncomfortable. Not easy.
Just real.

There was no apology.
No rehashing.
No carefully chosen words meant to explain away the silence of years.

Just two people fixing what they could,
in the only way either of us knew how.

And as the sun shifted across the yard, and the last board settled into
place, I felt something shift inside me too. Not a clean break or sudden
forgiveness—just a loosening.

A little more room where the anger used to live.

And when I looked up at the fence we'd mended together,
I realized: Not everything has to go back to the way it was.
Some things don't need to be what they once were to still hold.

Sometimes it's enough to meet in the middle.
To put something upright again, together.

To build from where you are—
and let that be the beginning.

# Let Go of the Need to Be Perfect.

Perfection is an illusion.
Embrace your flaws, mistakes, and learning curves
—they're all part of being human.
Aim for growth, not flawlessness.
Embrace Imperfection.

# This, Too, Is Living

I OFTEN FIND myself drifting back to that magical evening in Paris—the kind of memory that gets more cinematic every time I replay it. It was a warm summer night, and the air was thick with the scent of blooming jasmine and the distant hum of overly ambitious accordion players. I had spent the day ticking off tourist boxes—Louvre, croissant, existential dread—but the highlight was yet to come.

As the sun began to set, casting a golden glow over the Seine and making everything look suspiciously like a perfume ad, I made my way to the Eiffel Tower.

With a sense of childlike wonder (and an adult sense of knee pain from all the walking), I ascended the tower, each step bringing me closer to that overpriced, breathtaking view. When I reached the top, the city sprawled out beneath me—a sea of twinkling lights and old buildings that looked like they were built just to make your hometown feel shabby. The sight took my breath away. Not in the romantic sense. Literally. I was winded. There are a lot of steps.

A gentle breeze tousled my hair and, for a moment, the world paused. I could hear the distant laughter of couples, the clinking of wine glasses from cafes, and the soft murmur of the river below. I closed my eyes, soaking it all in. Paris seemed to lean in, whispering its secrets, and I felt like I was finally in on them. I felt truly alive.

Then, of course, the cat happened.

Just as I was reliving that dreamy Parisian bliss, the unwelcome, rather plump neighborhood cat—who I'm convinced belongs to someone rich and neglectful—took the opportunity of my open bedroom window to visit. With a soft thud, it landed on the windowsill like an entitled roommate who doesn't pay rent but insists on using your Netflix.

Its fur was a patchwork of orange and white, like it had been poorly quilted by a distracted grandmother. The cat's green eyes gleamed with curiosity—or judgment, honestly hard to tell. It meowed softly, as if to say, "You again?" and strutted in.

We glared at each other for a moment, but it wasn't a fair fight. The cat had the upper hand in confidence and emotional detachment. With the air of someone who knew this wasn't the first or last time it would ignore house rules, it settled on my bed like a fuzzy dictator.

Once, I had been the one striding into rooms like I owned them. I was a dancer. A traveler. A marathon runner. Then came the rainy Tuesday. I was late to a meeting—ironic, since I'd spent so much of my life trying to be present—and didn't see the car. It didn't miss me.

I woke up in the hospital with a broken body and a spirit that had apparently also taken the hit. Paralyzed from the waist down. The doctors said I was lucky. I wanted to punch them. With time, they said, I'd regain some movement in my arms and hands. I didn't feel lucky. I felt like the punchline of a joke the universe found particularly hilarious.

My life shrank. My friends visited less and posted more. The days were long, spent in a grand villa that echoed with my former adventures. It's amazing how a place can feel both luxurious and like a very well-decorated prison.

I hated the photos. Every wall, every shelf, a shrine to the old me. Laughing on a mountaintop. Hanging out of a helicopter. Jumping into oceans. Smiling, always smiling, as if the sheer force of my grin could bend life to my will.

Now, I understood why people scowled in old paintings. They got it.

I used to pity people in wheelchairs. How generous of me. Now, I was one of them. The irony was rich, and not the fun, "dark chocolate" kind of rich—the bitter, medicinal kind that lingers.

One evening, I stared too long at a photo of me crossing the New York City Marathon finish line, arms raised like a cliché. It felt like someone else's life—or maybe a prank someone had pulled by Photoshopping my face onto an inspirational poster. In a burst of rage, I grabbed the frame and flung it at the wall. It shattered. So did I, a little.

A few minutes later, my mother came in with groceries. She had moved across the country to help. She cleaned up the mess without saying much, sweeping up the glass with the quiet efficiency of a woman who has spent years saying things through actions instead of words.

Our relationship had always been a sitcom with no laugh track—dry, awkward, unresolved. I resented her for being there, and for not being there earlier. I hated how much I needed her, and how much she didn't ask whether I did.

"Thanks, Mom," I muttered, barely audible.

She looked up, nodded, and carried on like I'd said, "Please pass the salt."

"I'll make us some tea," she offered, her voice softer than usual. I nodded. Because what else could I say? Sorry for weaponizing nostalgia?

153

Then Jack entered.

Jack was my physical therapist—a sunny man with messy hair, a ridiculous sense of optimism, and a disturbing love for flaxseed. He had this annoying habit of being exactly what I needed, which only made me want to trip him. With my mind, since my legs had checked out.

From day one, Jack made it his personal mission to convince me that life wasn't over. I made it mine to convince him it absolutely was.

He smiled. I scowled. He complimented my progress. I grunted like an emotionally constipated raccoon.

At the end of each session, he'd wheel me into the garden, as if nature could heal spinal trauma and bitterness. The roses were blooming. The air smelled like life. I hated it. Every flower I picked with trembling fingers felt like an insult to who I had been—but also, maybe, a very slow, stubborn start to becoming someone new.

One afternoon, Jack surprised me with what he called "a little treat." I assumed it was another smoothie made of things that should never be blended, but no. He had arranged for a local violinist to play in the garden. My garden. For me.

The soft melodies drifted through the air like some indie film soundtrack I hadn't signed up for. I closed my eyes and let the music wash over me. For a moment, I wasn't in a wheelchair. I was twirling again, leaping with grace, limbs alive with rhythm. On the inside, I was humming along. On the outside, I crossed my arms and wore the expression of someone being subjected to a very classy hostage situation. Every time Jack glanced at me, I gave him a look that screamed, End this madness, Beethoven.

But Jack was undeterred. The man had the emotional endurance of a

Labrador retriever. He kept finding new ways to chip away at my fortress of gloom. Small adventures. Short trips into the nearby town. A forced march through joy, essentially.

He took me to the market, where the colors, smells, and chaotic energy of life almost tricked me into caring. Vendors shouted, fruit glittered in the sunlight like edible jewels, and some old man tried to sell me a handmade broom with "good luck" carved into the handle. (I didn't buy it. I was already sitting down all day—how much more luck did I need?)

We strolled by the lake. The water was calm, birds called in the distance, and I hated how beautiful it all was. It felt like the world was trying to seduce me with serenity. I was still mad. But my resistance was beginning to crack.

Then came The Boat Evening.

Jack was suspiciously excited. The kind of excited that usually results in someone getting wet.

The sun was low, the sky golden, and Jack revealed his plan: a small boat, covered in cushions like it was preparing for a Pinterest photoshoot, sat bobbing gently at the dock.

"Are you sure about this, Jack?" I asked, trying to sound skeptical instead of terrified.

He grinned. "Trust me, Emma. I haven't lost a patient yet."

"Yet," I muttered, eyeing the water like it owed me money.

With his usual gentle efficiency, he helped me into the boat. It rocked. I did not. But soon we were gliding across the lake, the water reflecting the sky in a way that would've made even my pre-accident self pause and say, "Okay, fine, it's pretty."

We floated past lilies and low-hanging trees while Jack rowed us toward a pocket of stillness in the middle of the lake. The air was warm and rich with summer. I closed my eyes and let the breeze touch my face like a soft hand I'd forgotten I missed.

"Look," Jack said.

I opened my eyes to a family of ducks swimming in formation like they were auditioning for a Disney short. I smiled. Like, really smiled. Unplanned and uncontrollable. Dammit.

Jack started talking about his childhood. Stories of fishing with his grandfather, full of nostalgia and detail that made it sound like a Norman Rockwell painting had come to life.

"There was this one time," he said, chuckling, "I was about eight. Finally felt a tug on the line. Pulled it up with all my might and… it was an old boot."

I snorted. "Did you cook it?"

"Worse," he grinned. "I made my grandpa hang it in the living room. Said it was my first catch. It's still there."

I laughed. A full, real laugh that startled even me.

It felt like finding a song I hadn't heard in years and realizing I still knew all the words. I laughed so hard I nearly forgot I hated sunshine, ducks, and Jack's unwavering cheer.

And just like that, the sadness loosened its grip—just a little.

Jack looked at me with that soft, smug smile of his. "See? There's still so much to laugh about, so much to live for."

He stopped rowing and let the boat drift. Then, he reached into his bag and pulled out a small wrapped bundle.

"I have something for you," he said, handing it over.

I looked at it like it might explode. "Unless it's chocolate, you're setting a high bar here."

It wasn't chocolate. It was a journal. A beautiful one, covered in intricate vines and pressed flowers. It looked like the kind of thing you'd find in a fairy tale, or on an overpriced Etsy store.

"I thought you might like to start writing again," Jack said, voice low and sincere. "To remember the beauty. To catch the moments before they float away."

Tears welled up—traitorous things. I looked at him, confused, suspicious, moved.

"How did you know I used to write?" I asked.

"I found one of your old notebooks," he admitted. "Read a few lines. Hope that's not creepy."

"It is," I said. "But also… thank you."

My voice cracked, thin and wet with emotion. It felt like unsealing something that had been locked for too long. A part of me I thought had drowned was suddenly gasping for air.

When Jack first came into my life, I wanted him gone. He was too shiny, too hopeful, too much. His "Good morning, Emma!" chirps were an assault on my preferred schedule of brooding in peace. I gave him nods so curt they were practically legal disclaimers.

But he kept showing up. Not pushy. Not dramatic. Just there. Like sunlight under a door you didn't realize had been cracked open.

Once, during a therapy session that was going terribly, Jack tried to encourage me.

"You're doing great," he said, chipper as always. "Just a little more effort and you'll see the progress."

I snapped. "Why do you even bother? I'm not getting better. This is all pointless."

He didn't flinch. Not even a blink. He looked at me and said, "I bother because I believe in you. Even when you don't. Especially then."

And just like that, the dam broke. I cried. I wept. Ugly, snotty, snot-that-defies-physics tears. And he didn't run. He sat beside me in silence, his presence steady and human. No pep talks. No clichés. Just quiet, which I think might be the loudest kind of love.

Over time, I began to notice the small, almost imperceptible ways he stitched comfort into the chaos of my days. The way he adjusted the pillows on my wheelchair like he was defusing a bomb—delicately, purposefully, with an expression of exaggerated focus that made me laugh despite myself. The way he brought me fresh flowers from the garden, often mismatched and occasionally accompanied by a bug or two—as if Mother Nature herself had personally delivered a cheerful, slightly unkempt bouquet. And most of all, the way he listened—really listened—without flinching or offering up motivational slogans like "Everything happens for a reason." He let me rage, cry, joke, and spiral without once trying to fix me.

It wasn't immediate, but eventually, my carefully constructed wall of sarcasm and scorn began to crack. Jack wasn't just some chipper caregiver on a mission to "bright-side" me to death. He was becoming something else. A friend. A safe place. The human equivalent of a weighted blanket and a bad pun.

When he entered the room now, something stirred inside me—a flicker of warmth, a pulse of something dangerously close to… hope. Jack reminded me that I wasn't entirely alone in this strange, unwanted second act of my life. He wasn't trying to drag me back to who I used to be; he was just here, helping me navigate the weird, uneven terrain of who I was now.

But healing isn't linear. It's more like a drunken game of hopscotch played blindfolded in the rain. Even on the best days, when Jack had me laughing so hard I forgot I was in a wheelchair, night would fall—and with it, the silence. The shadows. The memories. The ache. Jack would sleep, and I'd be left awake, stewing in my favorite bedtime cocktail: physical pain, existential dread, and a generous splash of self-loathing.

The truth is, before Jack, I had a plan. Not a five-year plan. A very different kind of plan. The kind that came with forms, signatures, and enough legal paperwork to make even the most hardened lawyer sweat. A tidy Swiss exit strategy, complete with complimentary sedation and a scenic mountain view. You know, the deluxe suffering-is-over package.

I hadn't told anyone, but like all good secrets, mine had a habit of showing up at the worst possible time. One day, a letter from the facility arrived. My mother opened it, of course. She has the boundaries of a raccoon in a pantry. Her face, when she read it, crumbled like a sandcastle in a tsunami. I'd never seen her cry like that—raw, unfiltered sorrow laced with a confusion that screamed, How did I not see this coming?

Despite our many misfires over the years—her hugs that felt like drive-by shootings, her pep talks that sounded like motivational ransom notes—I knew she loved me. She just didn't always know how to show it in a way I could absorb. Her reaction hit me harder than I'd expected. I'd tried so hard to control my exit, but in doing so, I forgot the collateral damage. Forgot that love, even awkward and misshapen, leaves deep footprints.

But the suicidal ideation didn't magically disappear after that confrontation. Jack didn't cure me—he paused me. He interrupted the spiral. Like someone sneaking in during a Netflix binge of my darkest thoughts and hitting pause right before the most devastating episode.

The guilt was relentless. How could I still feel hopeless when someone like Jack showed up every day with arms full of love, laughter, and way too much granola? But healing isn't gratitude. It's messier. You can be thankful and still wish the pain would end. You can laugh and still want to disappear. Two things can be true at once—and that's the cruelty of it.

Still, amid the inner chaos, some moments shone through like slivers of sunlight breaking through closed blinds. I remember the day I realized I wasn't just falling for Jack—I was already head-first, cartoon-style, heart-shaped-eyes in love with him.

It was a crisp autumn afternoon. One of those aggressively charming days where the air smells like cinnamon and the trees are doing their yearly impression of a firework show. Jack took me to an apple orchard he claimed was a childhood sacred site. He told me stories as we rolled between rows of trees, each tale more ridiculous than the last—like the time he tried to impress a girl by juggling apples and gave himself a concussion. I laughed until my stomach hurt.

As the sun dipped below the horizon, he brought me beneath a tall apple tree and said, "This one right here—this is the one I climbed when I was ten. My dad stood right where you are, yelling, 'You fall, you die!' Classic encouragement."

He handed me an apple, brushing a bit of dirt off like it was a precious gem. I took a bite, and in that moment, I felt it—the calm, the clarity, the terrifying awareness that this man, this glorified pillow-adjuster and trauma-interrupter, had become the epicenter of my emotional earthquake.

But love is a complicated guest when you don't even love yourself. I didn't want to tell him. What if he stayed out of guilt? What if I broke him the way I'd already broken myself? So I kept it to myself, tucked that truth into the folds of our shared days like a secret note I was too scared to pass.

It was beautiful. And it hurt like hell.

Then, one evening, everything shifted.

We were sitting by the fireplace, wrapped in a silence that felt heavier than any words could be. The fire cast a gentle, amber glow across the room, its flickering light dancing across Jack's face. The only sound was the quiet crackle of burning wood—so calm, so steady—while inside me, everything was unraveling. I stared into the flames, searching for some kind of courage in their movement. I couldn't bring myself to look at Jack, not yet. My chest ached with the weight of what I was about to say, and every tick of the clock behind us felt like it was counting down my secret.

Time was running out. And he didn't even know it.

My hands were clenched tightly in my lap, my fingers cold despite the fire's warmth. My heart pounded so loudly, it drowned out my thoughts.

"Jack," I said finally, my voice barely audible, "I... I need to tell you something."

He turned toward me slightly, sensing the shift in my tone. His face was calm, but I could see the tension in his jaw, the quiet readiness to listen.

I hesitated. The words felt too heavy, too final.

"I've been thinking about... leaving."

Jack's eyes widened, but he didn't speak. He just watched me, waiting, the weight of his attention grounding but terrifying.

I drew in a shaky breath, my whole body trembling. "I gave myself a deadline," I continued, voice cracking. "A window to tie up loose ends... before I go to Switzerland."

"Switzerland?" Jack repeated, confusion flickering across his face. "What are you talking about?"

I kept my gaze on the fire, unable to face the hurt I knew was forming in his eyes. "There's a place there," I whispered. "A facility... where people can make that choice. Where they let you go, peacefully. With dignity."

For a moment, there was no response—just the sound of the fire and the roaring in my ears.

Then Jack inhaled sharply. "Emma, no," he said, his voice trembling. "You can't be serious. You can't just... leave."

His words broke something open in me, the fear and pain I'd been holding back flooding forward all at once. But I still couldn't look at him —not yet.

Tears welled up in my eyes, hot and blinding. My voice cracked as I tried to speak through the tightness in my throat. "I don't want to leave, Jack," I whispered, each word a struggle. "But the pain... it's too much. Every day feels like a mountain I don't have the strength to climb. I can't keep living like this—not when everything that used to make life feel full has been taken from me."

Jack didn't rush in to comfort me. He didn't interrupt or try to fix it. He just listened—with a stillness that made me feel, for the first time in a long while, truly seen. His eyes didn't just show concern—they held me there, steady, patient, anchoring me while I broke apart. When I finally looked up, he reached for my hand. His touch was gentle, warm, grounding—like he was trying to hold the pieces of me together.

"Emma," he said, his voice low and tender, "life isn't just about what we can do. It's about who we are, and who we are to each other. It's the love we give, the laughter we still have left, the beauty that shows up in small, quiet ways—like this fire, or the way you still light up when you talk about books, or how you always know when someone else is hurting."

He leaned in a little closer, his voice firmer now, threaded with emotion. "You have so much to offer, Emma. So much left to feel, to give, to receive. Don't let the chair—or the pain—be the end of your story. Let it just be a chapter. A hard one, yes. But not the last."

I watched his face shift as he spoke—his usual calm replaced with something far more vulnerable. His eyes shimmered, glassy with tears he hadn't let fall. His brow was furrowed with emotion he could no longer keep locked away, and there was a raw, unfiltered honesty in his voice that shook me more than anything else could have.

He paused, and for a long moment, we just sat there in the space between what had been said and what hadn't. Then, he swallowed hard, his grip on my hand tightening ever so slightly.

"There's more," he said softly, almost like he was afraid of the weight his next words might carry.

I turned to him fully, my heart pounding so hard I felt it in my ears. "What is it, Jack?"

He took a slow breath, steadying himself before he spoke. And then, with a quiet bravery I didn't expect, he said, "I love you, Emma. I've loved you for a long time."

The air shifted—thicker now, charged with something both terrifying and beautiful.

"It breaks my heart to hear you talk like this," he continued. "Because I've spent all this time hoping—waiting—for the right moment to tell you. I can't imagine a world without you in it. I don't want to. And when your mom told me about your plan, I... I couldn't stay silent anymore. I told her how I felt. I had to. I thought maybe, just maybe, if you knew how much you mean to me... you might stay."

His voice cracked, but his eyes stayed on mine—wide open, vulnerable, pleading. He wasn't just offering love. He was offering a reason.

Jack paused, his gaze dropping to the floor as if the memory physically weighed him down. He rubbed the back of his neck, searching for the right words.

"One day," he began quietly, "you were in one of those dark places... one of the storms I never knew how to calm. I was standing outside your door, ready to come in and try to make you smile, maybe tell one of those dumb jokes you hate but secretly laugh at."

He gave a small, sad smile before continuing.

"But before I could knock, I saw your mom walking out—she was carrying a tray, and the food on it was untouched. Not a single bite. She closed the door gently, but the second she turned the corner, she collapsed into the chair by the stairs and… she just broke. She buried her face in her hands and started sobbing."

He swallowed hard, his voice beginning to tremble despite the steadiness he was trying to hold onto. "I couldn't just walk away. So I sat next to her. I asked what was wrong, and she said…" He paused, looking at me. "She said, 'She's going to do it, you know. She's given up. She doesn't want to live anymore.'"

My breath caught in my throat.

"I didn't know what to say," Jack continued, his voice softer now, almost reverent. "I just sat there, stunned. It felt like the ground had dropped out beneath me. But I told her the truth. I told her how I feel about you. That I've loved you for a long time. Longer than I ever let myself admit."

He looked at me, his eyes burning with unspoken things. "She was surprised, yeah. But she got it. And we both hoped—hoped so hard— that maybe if I told you… if you knew… maybe it would make a difference. Not just for me. For you. Because Emma, even when you couldn't see it, there was still so much light in you."

He took my hand again, this time with both of his, holding on like I was the only thing keeping him steady. "Please, Emma. Don't go. Stay. Stay with us. Stay with me."

His words hit me like a tide I couldn't brace against. A storm of love, sorrow, and guilt surged through me all at once. My chest ached from it.

He loved me. All this time, he had loved me—and I'd been so caught in my own pain, I hadn't even seen it. I had almost walked away from someone who saw the parts of me I thought were ruined and still wanted to stay. Tears spilled down my cheeks as I met his eyes, feeling cracked wide open. "I love you too, Jack," I whispered, my voice thick and shaking

"I've loved you for so long… but I was terrified. I didn't want to drag you down. I didn't want to be the reason your life got harder."

Jack shook his head fiercely, his grip firm and unwavering. "Emma, no. You're not a burden. You never were. You're the best thing that's ever happened to me. And I want to be here for all of it—the good, the hard, the in-between. I want you—not some perfect version. Just… you."

His words planted something in me that had been missing for so long— hope. Not the loud, blinding kind. But a quiet, steady flicker. The kind you find after being lost in the dark for too long.

And in that moment, I understood something I hadn't before: yes, Jack loved me, and yes, he would fight for me. But I had to do the same. For myself.

Because in the still moments—when Jack was asleep, or out running errands, or laughing with friends—I would be alone with me. And I had to believe I was worth staying for. I had to choose to live not just for love, or for the people who cared about me, but because somewhere deep inside, I still had something left. Something beautiful. Something worth saving.

I needed to find my way back to joy. Not the old kind—the new kind. A joy that could live alongside the pain. A joy that could be quiet, and small, and real.

And mine.

As the sun beamed through the windows on the first day of summer, I wheeled myself in front of the big floor-length mirror in our bedroom. It had been covered for months—by my order, of course. I had declared it a "No Sadness Zone" and banned any reflective surfaces that could sneak attack me with a glimpse of the dreaded recovery goblin I was convinced I had become. But not today. Today, I yanked off the white sheet like I was revealing a new car on a game show.

I looked up slowly, cautiously locking eyes with the woman staring back at me. Then I scanned every inch I could see. And to my surprise, I didn't look like a melted crayon left on a radiator. I looked... like me. Slightly thinner, sure. Maybe a little tired. But still me—just sitting down.

I began spinning slowly in front of the mirror, examining different angles, striking exaggerated poses, and making faces that could only be described as "mildly unhinged Muppet." I cracked myself up. "You know who still got it? Me, that's who," I said out loud. "Still a cutie. Still got the sauce."

Of course, this had to be the moment Jack chose to peek in.

His eyes widened. He blinked once, then again—like maybe I was a mirage conjured by leftover pizza dreams. Then he stepped out, only to re-enter dramatically with a theatrical gasp. "Am I hallucinating? Or did someone finally uncover the forbidden mirror of self-love?"

I burst out laughing. "Oh, you better believe it."

We both doubled over, the kind of laughter that makes your face hurt and your lungs wheeze. I rolled the sheet into a ball and chucked it at him, nailing him in the face like a towel-based Cupid's arrow. He staggered back, arms flailing, and fell onto the bed in surrender.

When the laughter faded, he looked at me—really looked at me—with so much tenderness it made my stomach flip. "You look amazing," he said softly. "I always knew you were beautiful. But seeing you see it... that's the most incredible part."

And that was it. That was the moment I believed it too.

That I was beautiful. That I was worthy. That I was enough.

Now, here I am. Paris again.

Not standing on the Eiffel Tower this time, but sitting—front-row seat to the best view in town. And no, I don't mean the cityscape. I mean Jack, across from me, with his ocean-colored eyes and his weird little cowlick that refuses to lie flat no matter how hard he tries. Candlelight flickers between us, and the scent of butter, wine, and destiny fills the air.

We're tucked into this tiny restaurant in Montmartre—where the décor looks like your grandma's attic mated with a jazz bar—and I love it. The waiter has a twinkle in his eye like he knows he's part of something big. Jack squeezes my hand and shifts in his seat like he's about to jump out of it.

My heart stumbles a little. Happy tears threaten. I already know what he's about to say. And I'm ready.

He looks at me, all nervous and glowing, and says, "Emma… there's something I've been meaning to ask you…"

And in my head, I whisper back, Let it be weird. Let it be sweet. Let it be ours.

Because joy lives here now. Right next to the pain. And it's not going anywhere.

# Nurture the Relationships that Nurture You

Invest in relationships that uplift,
respect, and support you.
Make time for genuine connection,
practice active listening,
and express appreciation often.

# To Look Life in the Face

To look life in the face
and know it—
truly know it—
for what it is.

To love it,
not despite the weight,
but because of it.

To feel the currents beneath the surface,
the quiet shifts between joy and grief,
the constant pull and push of being alive—
wild, untamed, and asking to be understood.

To carry the weight of endless nights,
the crushing silence when hope goes missing,
when the light dims to nothing
and you wonder if anyone would notice
if you disappeared.

That hollow echo in the dark,
where shadows cling like old regrets
and memories curl into themselves,
a universe within you that sighs—
empty, starless, vast.

To stand at the edge of giving up,
to feel the pull of letting go,
to question every breath you take
and ask, "Is this all there is?"

A fragile balance, stretched too thin,
where doubt takes root and whispers win.
But even in that trembling place,
there's something primal still awake—
the stubborn urge to seek the light.

And then—
a whisper cuts through the dark.
A flicker of warmth.
A memory of love.
A reason, however small,
to hold on.
To fight.

A fragile thread reaching out,
a knowing, soft and low,
that even in the darkest soil,
something can still grow.

To see the truth in every moment—
the silent passage of time,
the weight of every breath,
the depth of every sigh.

And in that truth, a paradox:
joy tangled up with sorrow,
a tapestry unfolding now,
woven with both beauty and burden.

To look life in the face
and know it.
To love it—
for what it is.

A journey worth enduring.
A story still unfolding.
A chance to find the beauty
in the smallest, hardest moments.

To see the dawn after the darkest night.
To feel the warmth of a new day breaking.
To hear laughter that shatters silence.
To find strength in the smallest kindness.

To let pain carve wisdom into your soul.
To find meaning in what you've survived.
To rise—not to escape the shadows,
but to see how strong you've become
by learning to carry them.

Each scar a story.
Each wound a testament
to what you've endured
and refused to let destroy you.

To hold on to threads of hope,
to weave them into something larger—
a tapestry of dreams,
a belief in tomorrow,
a trust in what's still possible.

Even fragile threads can hold.
Even darkness can't deny
the stubborn bloom beneath the sky.

To look life in the face
and know it.
To love it—
for what it is.

A testament to resilience.
A testament to grace.
A testament to the human spirit
that refuses to be erased.

# The Sweater

I FOUND IT folded on the top shelf of the closet I never go through. Tucked between an old winter coat and a box of tangled cords. Her sweater. The green one with the wooden buttons.

It still smells like her.

Not perfume—just that soft, clean warmth I could never name but always knew. Like laundry and patience. Like the hum of the dishwasher at night, or the way she'd touch my back when passing by, as if to say I see you without needing words.

I sit on the floor, cross-legged, the sweater in my lap like something sacred. I run my fingers over the hem. A little frayed. One button loose. The sleeve stretched where she used to tug at it when she was nervous.

She wore it the last time I saw her laugh without effort.
That kind of laughter that fills a room and then lingers in the corners, even after everything else has gone quiet.

I press it to my face. It's not enough, but somehow it is.

I don't cry. I thought I might, but I don't.

I just sit there, breathing in the space she used to fill. Letting the silence hold me the way she once did.

Remembering how much she gave, without asking for anything back.
How often I took that for granted. How many little things she made feel
safe.

And for the first time, I stop wishing I'd said more.

Because I think she knew.
Because she always knew.

And love like that doesn't vanish—it just lingers in cotton and memory
and quiet rooms. In the weight of a thing you thought you lost, waiting
quietly on a shelf.

I fold the sweater again, slowly, like it matters.
Like it deserves the care she gave everything.

And I place it back on the shelf.
Not to forget.
But to remember softly.

To let it be part of the quiet I carry forward.
The part that still feels like home.

be who you needed back then
or who you still need now
either way, someone out there could use
your kind of magic

# *Let Me Hate You*

Why was I cursed with this soul?
This brain that traps me in your pain,
This constant burden of understanding,
When all I want is to forget.
To feel nothing but my own rage—
Not your sorrow, not your regrets.

I don't want to feel sorry for you anymore.
I don't want to bury your scars under my skin,
Make them my own.
I don't want to keep seeing your face in my reflection
When I close my eyes—
I want to hate you.

I want to suffocate in it.
To be swallowed whole by this fire,
To feel it burn through my veins
Until I'm an unrecognizable molten core of rage and
disgust.
Let me scream your name, your sins into the night
until it feels like a curse
That wraps around me tighter than my skin.
Let the darkness consume me—
And leave me with nothing but this blackened heart
That has only one purpose: vengeance.

Is that too much to ask?

Why does it have to be this way?
Why do I have to be the one
Who can't even feel my own wounds,
While I keep collecting yours like they're trophies?
Why can't I just destroy everything in my path?
Why can't I be heartless like you?
Why do I still care?

But no...
No matter how deeply I sink,
No matter how much I claw at the walls of my rage,
The light finds me.
It pulls me out of the abyss,
Like I don't have the right to sit in my own sorrow.
Makes me reach for something I don't want anymore.
Something weak.
Something forgiving.

And it makes me wonder—
Why?
Why am I cursed to remember your suffering
Before I even had words?
Why do I feel your hollow ache
That was never meant to be mine?
Before I could understand anything,
I understood you—
Understood what it was like to be broken
But not know how to shatter.

So here I am,
Trapped in this ridiculous cycle of mercy,

When all I want to do is burn.
And yet, even when I could've turned away,
I still chose to love you—
Not because I should,
But because you couldn't choose to love yourself.

I wanted to rescue you—
To take your broken pieces and make them whole.
But now I realize:
I was never meant to fix you.
I was just the casualty of your war.

I see your face sometimes
In the flicker of shadows,
In the quiet spaces where nobody dares to go.
And I wish I could forget you.
I wish I could scrub you out of my veins,
Erase you from my body and mind.
But your pain... it sticks to me.

You hurt me.
And you'll never know how much.
You'll never know the quiet screams I swallowed
To keep your suffering at bay.
And I mourn that.
I mourn what I lost and what you never had
And therefore, could never give.
And it aches—
A deeper ache than any grief I've ever felt.
I wish I could scream it,
Wish I could let it all out,

But it's like there's a dam built inside me,
And it just keeps holding back my own damn tears.

I want to be heartless,
I want to feed your suffering to the flames
Until all that's left is ash.
But it's not me.
It never will be.
And God help me, I hate that.
I hate that I was made to feel,
To heal, to forgive
When all I want is to feel the release
Of letting go of the weight you left me with.

I wanted to drown in the darkness.
But I was built for light.
So I forgive you,
Not because you deserve it,
But because I would choke on the bitterness
If I didn't.

I'm not angry anymore that I couldn't save you.
Or her.
Or anyone.

I was never meant to.
There's only One who could.

But before your eyes close—
Before you slip into whatever abyss awaits you—
I pray that somewhere in your final breath,
You feel the weight of real kindness.
And just maybe—just maybe—
You'll finally recognize it.

Because I know what it's like
To be unseen, unloved, misunderstood—
And still, against all the odds, choose love anyway.

I chose love.
And even now, even after everything,
In the middle of this chaos,
I still do.

healing isn't always gentle sometimes it's
the war you wage within yourself to stay
soft in a world that taught you to burn

# Lost Dog, Found Self

IT WAS SUPPOSED to be easy.

Feed the dog. Walk the dog. Keep the dog alive for 72 hours while my neighbor visited her boyfriend in Santa Fe or Sedona or somewhere with desert energy and artisanal pickles.

I agreed because I thought it might help me re-enter the world gently. A dog is manageable. A dog doesn't ask questions like, What have you been working on lately? or Are you still painting?

Spoiler: I was not. I hadn't touched a pencil in months. The idea of creating anything made my insides go very still, like when you hear a strange noise in your apartment and pretend you didn't.

Anyway. The dog's name was Churro. Small, shaggy, and somehow always slightly damp.

And I lost him.

One second he was sniffing a bush. The next—gone. Like Houdini, but smellier.

What followed was three hours of pure chaos: me running through the neighborhood in paint-stained sweatpants, calling "Churro!" with the rising panic of someone who knows they will absolutely never be trusted with anything living again. I even asked a man at a hot dog cart if he'd seen a small dog, which in hindsight was a ridiculous thing to do, considering the menu.

I checked the park. I checked alleyways. I considered crying behind a dumpster, but decided I wasn't quite ready for that milestone yet.

Instead, I kept walking—farther than I normally would. Past the bookstore I used to visit. Past the mural I'd once helped paint, now faded and tagged over. Past places I'd quietly erased from my map after everything got… hard.

And then, because the universe is deeply committed to irony, I found Churro. In a bakery. Sitting like a little cryptid in front of the pastry case, tail wagging, fully unbothered. The staff had given him a piece of croissant and named him "Assistant Manager."

I didn't know whether to laugh or faint, so I bought a scone and sat on the curb next to him. He licked my hand like I'd done something brave. Like I hadn't spent the last few hours spiraling through guilt, failure, and Craigslist ads for identical dogs.

We walked home slowly.

That night, I stared at my sketchbook for a long time. My hand felt stiff when I finally picked up the pencil, fingers slow to remember the weight. But I drew him anyway. Not well. Just loose lines, quick and uncertain. Something stretched in my chest.

I drew him again the next day. Then something else. Then something just for me.

My neighbor came home glowing with vacation smugness, thanked me and tossed her keys in a bowl like her dog hadn't been five streets away playing retail mascot.

But that's okay. Because Churro came back.
And so did I.

# The Boy in the Aisle

I RAN INTO him in the frozen food aisle. Of all places.

I didn't notice him at first—just a man reaching for a bag of peas, laughing into his phone. It was the laugh that caught me. Something in the back of my ribs tightened, that old reflex. Then he turned.

And there he was.

For a second, I expected the rush—rage, panic, maybe even the kind of cold numbness that used to carry me through whole months. But it didn't come. Just stillness. Almost curiosity.

He blinked, surprised. "Hey. Wow. You look… good."

I said thank you, and I meant it. We stood there, surrounded by waffles and steamable broccoli, making small talk like people who used to be something and now aren't anything at all.

He told me about his job, some band he's trying to start, how his dog died last year. I nodded, asked the right questions, smiled. There was a moment—just one—where he looked tired in a way that felt familiar. Eyes flickering with something unspoken. The weight of a story he still doesn't know how to tell.

I saw it then, not with my mind but with something deeper: the boy inside him, broken long before I met him, still trying to claw his way out through anger and control and fists. And I just… felt sorry. Not in a pitying way, but in the way you feel watching someone build a home out of rubble and never realize why the roof keeps falling in.

When we said goodbye, I didn't look back.

I got in my car, shut the door, and waited for the crash of emotions that never came. No hate. No fear. No imaginary monologue of things I wished I'd said.

Just a quiet breath, like one I'd been holding for years without realizing it.

I turned the key, and with the engine's hum came the softest kind of knowing:

I'm free.

Not because justice found me.
Not because he changed.
Because I did.

# *Off-Center*

Something shifted.
Parts of me don't sit like they used to.
Angles sharper,
curves louder,
movement a little more uncertain.

After the fall —
the shift that didn't kill me —
I returned,
not quite the same.

The mirror doesn't lie,
but it doesn't tell the full truth either.
What it reflects is
off-center.
Like it's remembering the shape I was
and trying to make sense of what I became.

People say,
"You're lucky."
And I am.
Luckier than some,
blessed even —
to be here,
to be mostly whole,
to still reach for things,
laugh with breath in my lungs.

But some days, I look at my reflection
and think,
This is what survival looks like?
Bent.
Heavy.
Quietly out of place.

I tell myself I shouldn't feel this way.
Others have it worse.
Much worse.
People are losing more than symmetry.
They're losing freedom.
Limbs.
Voice.
Lives.
Loved ones.
Minds.
Hope.

So who am I to mourn an old version of myself
when I'm still here?

But pain —
pain doesn't check headlines before it settles in.
It just arrives.
Uninvited.
Pulls up a chair,
sets the weight down
right in your chest.

And healing?
Healing is slow.

Soft.
Sometimes silent.
It whispers when I want answers.
It lingers when I want closure.

I'm not ungrateful.
I'm just...
adjusting.

To this version.
To this skin.
To this strange, unfinished chapter
where nothing is wrong enough to break me,
but nothing feels quite right either.

This isn't pity.
It's not self-hate.
It's the ache —
the low hum of being offbeat in your own body
while the world spins fast around you.

I'm learning to sit with it.
Not fix it.
Not justify it.
Just name it.
Gently.
So it doesn't grow sharper in the dark.

Because maybe
the healing happens
in the saying.

some days,
you'll rise with the light —
hope steady in your chest,
feet sure beneath you

other days,
you'll feel the weight return —
soft but heavy,
a quiet ache that asks to be named

this is not weakness.
this is not failure

it's just healing —
uneven,
honest,
real

you are not lost
you are becoming

# Grief Group and the Angry Muffin Lady

I DIDN'T WANT to be there.

The fluorescent lights buzzed like they hated everyone equally, and someone had arranged the chairs in a perfect, soul-sucking circle. I sat down anyway.

It was either this or cry in the grocery store again. The cereal aisle was starting to feel like enemy territory.

Everyone brought something to share—memories, tears, awkward silences. And one woman brought muffins. Bran. Dry as a confession. Every week. Like grief wasn't bad enough, now we had to chew sawdust.

I started calling her The Angry Muffin Lady in my head. She had that look, you know? Like she'd stared directly at God and wasn't impressed.

Week three, I made the mistake of joking, "Maybe next time we try chocolate chips?"

She stared at me like I'd insulted her dead husband. Maybe I had.

Week five, though—there were chocolate chips. Just a few. Buried in the middle like a secret. I bit into one and blinked. Not exactly good, but... something.

We didn't talk much—just exchanged polite nods, grief's version of a handshake. But I started looking forward to seeing her.

Something about her sharpness made me feel more real, less like a sad fog with shoes.

Then one day, she sat next to me.

Didn't say anything for a while. Just passed me a muffin and muttered, "I hated baking. He used to do it."

I nodded. "I hated Tuesdays. Now I just sit in a circle and eat your weird muffins."

She huffed. Might've been a laugh.

"His name was Arthur," she said. "He used to get up at 5 a.m. just to make these before work. He said muffins could fix anything. I told him that was ridiculous."

"Was he right?" I asked.

She shrugged. "I still don't know."

I told her about my sister—how she used to sing to plants, like that was going to help them grow. How the silence in my apartment now feels like it's watching me. I hadn't said her name out loud in weeks. It was like I'd been storing it behind my teeth. Saying it felt like pulling a splinter.

"My son used to call me 'Captain Serious,'" another guy in the group had said once. "Now I'd give anything to hear him roll his eyes again."

One man still wore his wife's old flannel, every week, no matter how hot it got. He said it still smelled like her. "Like cedar and lavender and someone who knew how to love me right."

Everyone had someone. Everyone had no one.

But the circle, somehow, held.

We never became best friends, the Muffin Lady and I. That's not how this works. But we sat next to each other every week. Sometimes we even talked. Once, we skipped group and went to a diner where the muffins were actually good. She told me Arthur would've hated them—too sweet, too soft. I told her my sister would've ordered two, just for the frosting.

Grief didn't leave. It just changed shape. Grew quieter. Less like drowning, more like a limp you forget about until the rain hits.

And the muffins got better.

# Cactus in the Office

I DIDN'T MEAN to notice it.

It sat there, quietly defiant, in the corner of my desk. A small thing in a too-bright ceramic pot, half-hidden behind a stack of reports I hadn't touched in three days.

No water. No sunlight. No attention.

And yet, it survived.

I leaned back in my chair, tapping my pen against the edge of the desk. The fluorescent lights hummed above me, casting that sharp, unnatural glow that made everything look a little too lifeless. The air smelled faintly of stale coffee and printer ink—an atmosphere built for function, not survival.

"Still alive?"

I glanced up. Claire from marketing, holding a coffee mug that announced "Mondays are canceled" in tired, chipping font.

"The plant or me?" I asked, nudging the cactus with my finger.

Claire snorted. "Both, honestly. But the cactus has better hair today."

She perched on the edge of my desk, eyes flicking between me and the plant, like she was trying to figure out which of us needed the HR Wellness newsletter more.

"Do you water it?"

I shrugged. "Haven't in weeks."

She raised an eyebrow. "And yet, it's thriving."

Thriving wasn't the right word. It was surviving. Keeping its edges sharp. Existing despite the environment—not because of it.

I traced a finger along one of its spines, careful not to press too hard.

Claire sipped her coffee, watching me. "Maybe that's the trick," she said finally. "Not needing much. Just taking whatever scraps life throws your way and not dying dramatically about it."

I hummed in response, staring at the cactus again.

Resilience looked different on everyone. Some people were houseplants —needing care, attention, the right conditions to flourish. Others were weeds, growing wildly, uninvited, bending without breaking.

And then, there were the cacti. The ones that built their armor in silence and waited.

Later, at lunch, when another coworker makes a cutting remark—too sharp, too precise, aimed at a wound I haven't quite healed from—I feel the usual instinct to shrink back, to let it slide without pushing against it.

But something stops me.

I think about the cactus. How it doesn't beg for gentleness or permission. How it doesn't wither in the absence of ideal conditions.

Something in me straightens. My edges feel a little sharper too.

I don't fire back. I don't escalate. But I don't shrink.

I hold my ground—just enough to remind myself that I am still here, still standing.

Still sharp.

And as I walk back to my desk, I glance at the little ceramic pot in the corner.

I meant to notice it this time.

# The Coffee is Perfect Today

I TAKE A sip. And it's perfect.

Not good, not decent, not passable enough to tolerate existence.
Perfect.

The kind of perfect that makes me pause mid-sip, reevaluate my entire day, and briefly suspect I might be in a commercial for inner peace.

I set the cup down, staring at the rich swirl of color against the ceramic rim. The steam curls upward, slow and deliberate, like it trained for this moment in a monastery.

The balance is exactly right—bold but not bitter, smooth but not weak. Just enough heat to warm my hands without scalding me into immediate regret.

I take another sip, closing my eyes for just a second.

It tastes like resilience. Like a small mercy from the universe. Like the first good decision I've made since cutting my own bangs during a quarter-life crisis.

This coffee is the kind of miracle that could solve global conflict. I briefly consider writing an email to world leaders, urging them to stop whatever they're doing and just…try this exact ratio of beans to cream.

Another sip.

A sigh.

A long, satisfied exhale that feels like setting down a heavy emotional suitcase I didn't even realize I was carrying.

Which, naturally, is when the universe notices I'm enjoying myself.

Balance must be restored.
Joy cannot go unpunished.

I reach for my laptop, fully prepared to channel this caffeinated clarity into something productive, and my elbow—my own elbow, the traitor—goes rogue.

One clumsy nudge, one tragic arc of physics, and suddenly—chaos.

The cup tips. The coffee spills. The divine becomes a puddle.

The steam disappears. The universe laughs.

I close my eyes again. This time, not out of joy, but grief.

Maybe tomorrow, another cup will save me.
Or at least not betray me.

# Prioritize Yourself Without Apology

Self-care is essential, not indulgent.
Listen to your needs—physical, emotional, spiritual
—and meet them with kindness,
not shame.

# Paper Mirrors, Steel Forks

THE DINING HALL hummed with the soundtrack of soft chatter, clinking cutlery, and the occasional awkward cough—like a symphony composed by anxiety and restraint. I sat at the long table, staring at the tray in front of me like it was a ticking time bomb covered in cheese. It was Fear Foods Night, or as I privately called it, Welcome to Your Personal Hell Buffet.

Tonight's line-up of terror? A slice of pizza (extra melty, extra mocking), a small bowl of pasta that looked too smug in its creamy glory, a deceptively innocent piece of chocolate cake, and—cue dramatic music —a glass of whole milk. Whole. Freaking. Milk. The horror.

Sarah, my favorite counselor and part-time food therapist/full-time human Prozac, appeared beside me. "Take your time, Emma," she said with the gentle patience of someone who has seen it all and still chooses hope. "Remember, you're in control."

In control? I thought. That's funny, considering I had just spent the last ten years being held hostage by a voice in my head that made Regina George seem like a motivational speaker.

I picked up the pizza slice. It stared back at me like it knew all my secrets. I could hear The Voice, that relentless inner saboteur, whispering like an overbearing aunt at Thanksgiving: "Are you sure you need all that cheese?" My hands trembled. I put it down. Cue dramatic sigh and internal monologue spiral.

Sarah noticed and leaned closer. "Try the pasta?" she offered gently.

200

"Just one bite."

The pasta looked... creamy. Like, French movie-level creamy. I dipped my fork in and licked it like it was poison, savoring the rich taste with the drama of someone performing an Oscar-worthy slow death scene. Sarah arched a brow. "Chewing helps, Emma."

Okay, fine. I twirled a forkful, brought it to my mouth, and chewed like a war hero returning from battle. Swallowed. Survived. My stomach didn't explode, no one fainted, and God didn't smite me for consuming carbs. A win.

Then came the chocolate cake. I used to love chocolate cake. When I was eight, I'd eat it with my fingers and giggle like a maniac. Now, I looked at it like it was made of plutonium. Still, I took a bite. Not a polite nibble—a real forkful. It tasted like memories, like birthdays and stolen frosting and messy joy. My brain tried to protest, but I tuned it out with a mental "Shhh... Let me have this one."

The milk, though? The milk was a monster. I'd trained myself to fear it. Skim milk was my toxic bestie—bland, pointless, but predictably safe. Whole milk was like inviting a leather-jacketed rebel into your life. I stared it down. Nope. Couldn't do it. I drank water instead, feeling like I'd just survived a gladiator match.

But Sarah wasn't giving up. "Emma," she said quietly, "if you don't start taking this seriously, we might have to resort to a feeding tube." She let that sink in, her voice soft but firm. "We don't want that. I know you don't either."

A shiver ran down my spine. A tube up my nose was not the TikTok content I had in mind for my future. I nodded. Message received.

As I sat there, shame and sadness tangled like headphone wires in my chest, my mind wandered back to where this all began.

I was twelve. I had a mirror, a magazine, and a brain that decided it hated me.

The mirror was a jerk. It pointed out every perceived flaw, turning molehills into Mount Everest. The voice was subtle at first, like a mean girl whispering behind my back. "You're not enough," it said. "You'll never be beautiful." Soon it wasn't whispering. It was screaming.

Food became the enemy. Hunger became an achievement. Compliments became fuel. "Wow, you lost weight!" they'd say, not realizing they were applauding the unraveling of a girl turning into a ghost. I wore baggy sweaters in July and said I was "just cold." I skipped meals and called it "intermittent fasting" before it was a trend.

The emptiness felt like power—until it didn't.

By the time I realized I couldn't stop, it was too late. I was a shell, running on caffeine and denial. My hair fell out like autumn leaves. My period ghosted me. My heart sometimes forgot how to beat properly. The voice was still there, now meaner, more urgent: "You're almost there. Don't quit now."

It was my mom who finally broke through.

She sat on the edge of my bed, voice cracking. "I love you," she whispered. "And I can't keep watching you disappear."

Something cracked in me. Not dramatically, just... enough. The next day, we saw Dr. Patel, who wore sensible shoes and had the calmest energy I'd ever seen. She didn't fix me. But she saw me. For the first time in a long time, someone saw past the weight and the lies and just saw... me.

Then came the intervention—my family huddled in a circle of desperate love. My dad looked like he hadn't cried since 1994, and yet here he was, holding my hand with wet eyes. My little sister, Emily, wouldn't even hug me anymore. She used to cling to me like a koala. Her love language was touch, and I had become untouchable. That broke me.

"I miss you," she whispered.

That was it. That was the moment. Screw the voice. I wanted hugs again.

Back in the dining hall, I looked at the fear food tray. I imagined my mom's cookies, my dad's dad-jokes, and Emily's arms wrapped around me. I took a deep breath, then bit into the pizza like it had insulted my family. I ate some pasta, more cake, even drank some milk—the whole milk. Okay, half. But still. Huge.

Sarah beamed. "I'm so proud of you."

And for once, I didn't flinch from the praise.

Each day after that was a rollercoaster—some ups, some stomach-dropping lows, but less fear. More freedom. I even started cracking jokes again during group therapy. Like the time I told the new girl that the cake here could double as a doorstop. We laughed. It felt good to laugh again.

Eventually, I got stronger. Literally. I started lifting weights—not to shrink, but to feel powerful. Who knew lifting heavy things could feel more rebellious than starving yourself?

My friends welcomed me back like I'd returned from war. They didn't tiptoe. They hugged hard, laughed loud, and let me cry when I needed to. Jessica sent me daily Baby Yoda memes during treatment. I still have a folder of them on my phone called "Yoda One For Me."

The recovery road is messy. It's full of detours, breakdowns, and the occasional emotional car fire. But I keep walking.

These days, I speak at schools and support groups. I tell people, "Don't wait until your hair falls out to ask for help." That usually gets a laugh. Dark humor's a survival tool—it lets us open wounds with a wince and a grin.

If you're reading this and struggling, please hear me:
You are not alone. You don't need to earn your meals, your rest, or your joy. You were never too much. You were never not enough. You are not a number. Not a project. Not a reflection warped by paper-thin lies.

**You are allowed to take up space.**
**To eat.**
**To heal.**
**To stay.**

And food? Food is not the enemy. **Fear is.**

The mirror may still lie some days, and the fork may still feel heavy—but each time you pick it up with courage, you shatter a little more of the illusion.

**You're stronger than the voice in your head.**
**You're made of steel.**
**And you are healing.**

**One bite, one truth, one day at a time.**

# Unseen Gifts

The storm raged fierce, the branches tossed,
I thought that all my light was lost.
But when the clouds began to break,
A quiet strength rose in their wake.

The path grew steep, the climb was long,
I stumbled hard, but still moved on.
And looking back, I clearly see—
The resilience carved inside of me.

The silence fell, a heavy weight,
I felt alone, adrift in fate.
But in that stillness, I could hear
A wiser voice, dissolving fear.

So thank you, trials, fierce and true,
For hidden gifts I never knew—
The strength revealed, the scars that mend,
A grateful heart that learns to bend.

the human heart doesn't
come with a doorknob
it's a weird little cave that only opens
from the inside

# The Plant That Wouldn't Die

I TRIED TO kill it. I really did.

It was his favorite plant—some smug little succulent with plump green leaves and a ridiculous name I could never remember. He bought it from one of those overpriced hipster shops where everything smells like eucalyptus and regret. He used to talk to it, like it was a person. I used to think it was cute.

I no longer think it's cute.

After he left, it sat on the windowsill like it owned the place. Bright and thriving and completely unbothered, like it hadn't lived in the same room where we yelled at each other about dishes and emotional availability.

So, I stopped watering it. Left the blinds shut. Let the dust settle thick on its leaves like ash.

Three weeks later, it looked better than me.

So then I moved it to the bathroom—no sun, constant humidity, and frankly, a sinister energy. It flourished. Grew a new leaf. Bastard.

I tried knocking it over "accidentally" (twice), but it barely noticed. I even whispered, "I hope you die," while brushing my teeth one morning, and it just sat there. Mocking me. Photosynthesizing like it had nothing better to do.

Eventually, I gave up.

Not in a dramatic, throw-it-out-the-window way—though I considered that—but more in a tired sigh kind of way. I started cracking the window open again. I wiped off its dusty little face. One day, without meaning to, I watered it.

Just once.

Then again.

Then, one day, I sat down on the edge of the tub and said, "You know, I think I miss hating him."

The plant didn't respond, obviously. It's not that kind of story.

But I kept talking anyway. Little things, nothing dramatic. Just thoughts I didn't have anywhere else to put. Things I didn't want to say out loud to actual humans. Like how I couldn't decide if I was lonely or just bored. Or how I secretly liked watching garbage reality TV because everyone was a disaster and it made me feel like maybe I was doing okay.

The plant listened. Or it didn't. But either way, it stayed alive.

So did I.

Now it lives by the kitchen window. I bought it a nicer pot—ceramic, navy blue, on sale. I still don't know what it's called. But sometimes I say good morning. Sometimes I even say thank you.

I water it once a week. Give or take.

And lately, I've started remembering to water myself, too.

# The Weight in My Hands

THERE'S A WEIGHT in my hands. Heavy—not unbearable, just… unexpected. Like I've been carrying it a long time without noticing, and only now, in this stillness, do I feel it. I look down. Shards. My palms are cupped, cradling jagged, uneven pieces. Some glint with a faded sheen, others are dull and cracked. Dust clings to them, like they've been buried or forgotten. My first instinct is to drop them—why am I holding this? Why now?

But something stops me.

I kneel, slowly. The floor feels cool and grounding beneath me. I set the pieces down, one by one, arranging them without really knowing why. My fingers move on their own, as if they remember something my mind hasn't caught up to.

There's a rhythm to it. A pull. Like solving a puzzle that was once whole and loved, shattered and discarded, yet still calling to be known.

The more I piece together, the more I recognize the shape. Not logically—emotionally. Viscerally. It's not just a thing. It's… familiar. Precious. The curve of a laugh, the edge of a memory. The ache of things I thought I'd lost. I feel my breath catch.

It's me.

The realization breaks over me, quiet and seismic. These shards… they're parts of myself. Every part I buried. Every part I broke. Every time I said, "I'm fine" when I wasn't. Every time I silenced a scream, swallowed grief, let my voice crack under someone else's weight. Every truth I made small. They're all here.

I feel a swell in my chest—not tears exactly, but close. Not grief exactly, but real or maybe just wonder. I'm not sure.

Piece by piece, I keep going. There's no blueprint, no perfection. Some shards fit awkwardly, not like they used to. Some never will. Others are missing. I don't force them. I just let it become. The edges don't smooth. They remain sharp, but they catch the light in beautiful ways. I start to see the veins—thin lines where the breaks once were, now rejoined. Like scars that refuse to fade.

It's not how I used to be. It's not clean, symmetrical, polished, new or even pretty.

But it's whole.
It's beautiful.
It's true.

Wabi-sabi.
The art of broken things made sacred.
The masterpiece made
after the breaking.
Not in spite of it.
Because of it.
I never understood it until now—until I became it.

I lift the reassembled form—myself—rebuilt, raw, radiant—and hold it close. The weight is still there. But it's different. It's earned. It's mine.

And for the first time in a long, long while…

I feel strong enough to carry it.

# Between Stops

THE BUS EXHALES at my stop with a hiss, swallowing me into its dim, hum-ming belly. I slide into a cracked leather seat near the back, where the overhead vents breathe warm air down my neck.

The scent is familiar: damp wool, burnt coffee, and someone's fading floral perfume fighting to stay alive.

My fingers are cold despite my gloves. I clutch my tote like a lifeline.

The city moves past in a blur of grey and smudged yellow—wet sidewalks reflecting neon, sleepy cafés with fogged-up windows, tired people blinking into the day. A man in a puffy coat nods off against the glass, his breath fogging the window in slow, steady pulses. A woman in a sharp blazer and pristine white sneakers taps furiously on her phone, her crimson nails flashing like warning lights.

They all look like they're headed somewhere that matters. Like they belong.

*Unlike me.*

I hear my mother's voice from last night, still echoing:
"All that talent, wasted. You could've been something."

As if I'm nothing now.
As if making someone smile because a dress finally fits right doesn't count for anything.

Her words sit in my chest like stones dragged from deep water.

I shrink into my navy coat, my bun coming loose at the edges. Even the bus feels like it's overlooking me. I glance down at my hands—chipped polish, half-moons of tired skin—and whisper,
What am I even doing with my life?

That's when I see her.

Across from me, a girl with wild curls tucked under a mustard beanie, sipping from a chipped thermos. She's curled into a paperback, lost in some other world. But it's her shirt that catches me—black cotton, threadbare, the lettering worn thin.

**"You are not a project. You are already whole."**

My breath catches.

It's not flashy. Probably thrifted. But the words hit like a doorway swinging open in my chest. I read them again. And again. The sting in my eyes surprises me.

She doesn't notice me watching. Still, I stare—as if I've just remembered something I buried long ago. Something small. Quiet. And stubborn.

I let it bloom.

The bus rounds a corner. The sun flashes off a puddle like a gold coin.

My stop is next.

And suddenly, I don't feel quite so heavy.

# The Spoon Theory In Action

I STARE AT the sink. The dishes stare back. A silent standoff.

The spoon in my hand is slick with soap, catching the overhead light in its curved reflection—a small crescent moon against the dull backdrop of abandoned plates and half-empty mugs.

It occurs to me, all at once, that I am out of spoons.

Literally.
Metaphorically.
Spiritually.
Emotionally.
Existentially.
**All of them.**

I have spent the day being functional, stretching myself thin across conversations, expectations, and an alarming number of "quick favors." My energy is a frayed thread, unraveling with every movement, every group chat reply, every "no worries if not" that absolutely was a worry.

I turn the spoon over in my palm. It's heavier than it should be. Possibly forged in the fires of burnout.

I *should* finish the dishes. I *should* cook something decent. I *should* rejoin society as a productive adult who uses oven-safe cookware for meals that don't come in boxes.

213

But the weight of **should** has been pressing against my ribs all day, and suddenly, I know—there is nothing left to give. Not to this sink. Not to these dishes. Not to the gods of adulthood who demand quinoa.

The faucet drips. The fridge hums. The universe is unimpressed by my dramatic inner monologue.

I rinse the spoon, dry it off with the corner of my sleeve (because the dish towel is, of course, also in the sink), and reach for the cereal box on the counter.

And just like that, the decision is made.

Not a failure.
Not surrender.
Just survival, in the form of sugar-coated resilience.

I pour the cereal, watch the milk swirl into the bowl, listen to the soft crackle of grains absorbing whatever dignity I have left. I take a bite, the cold sweetness settling against my tongue like reassurance from a childhood friend who never expected too much.

Tomorrow *might* be different.
**Or maybe not**.
But tonight,
I have **exactly one** spoon.
And I make do,
even when I **shouldn't** have to.

# Stationary Moon

THE HIGHWAY HUMS beneath us, a low endless sound like the world sighing. Streetlights blur into long gold streaks across the windshield. I'm curled up in the backseat, cheek pressed to the window, my breath fogging up a small patch of glass that I keep wiping clear with the sleeve of my hoodie.

It's late. Or early. The kind of time when everything feels softer and farther away.

Mom and Dad aren't speaking. They haven't for most of the drive. The radio plays something slow and forgettable, and the dashboard glows faint blue in the dark.

Out the window, the moon follows us.

It hangs in the sky like it's tied to the car, always just out of reach. Sometimes it disappears behind trees or gas station roofs, but it always comes back. Like it knows I'm watching.

I try not to cry. Not because I'm too tough, but because it won't change anything. The new apartment smells weird. The boxes in my room aren't unpacked. My old friends are two hundred miles behind us, like they were part of some life that just got cut off mid-sentence.

But the moon's still there.

I press my forehead to the glass, watching it follow us, mile after mile. Still glowing. Still moving without moving. I stare at it until my eyes blur, until the quiet inside the car matches the quiet in my chest. Always just there.

It's nothing, really. Just light and distance. Just a rock in the sky.

But it's the only thing that hasn't left.

And for some reason, that steadiness feels like a promise.

Like maybe I'm not as alone as I thought.

Like maybe something out there sees me, too.

# Blue Light in the Bathroom

THE MIRROR VIBRATES faintly with the light above it—a cold, flickering blue that makes everything look a little more ghost than flesh. I don't usually look at myself in this light.

Not closely. Not lately.

But tonight, I do.

Steam curls lazily at the edges of the glass, softening the corners of my reflection. My hair is damp, curling in defiance, and my skin—washed bare—feels thinner somehow, like paper after rain. I lean in. The eyes looking back are mine, but quieter. Older. Still here.

I open the drawer and pause. I know what I'm looking for. It's buried beneath expired coupons and dried-out mascara—one tube, scarlet and gold, worn smooth from years of being held.

The cap clicks open with a sound so familiar it startles something in me.

I haven't worn lipstick in months. Maybe longer. There wasn't a moment I stopped, just a slow forgetting. Days blurred into chores, nights into silence. Grief doesn't always announce itself. Sometimes it just...sits, quiet and patient, until you forget what it felt like to be anything else.

But tonight, something stubborn in me stirs. Not hope exactly. Not yet. Just the ache of wanting.

I bring the tube to my lips. The first swipe is tentative—waxy, dry—but the color is still rich. A little too bright for this lighting, maybe, but I keep going, smoothing the edges with my finger like I used to. I don't smile. Not quite. But something shifts.

The woman in the mirror isn't whole. She isn't glowing or transformed. She's tired. She's wearing an old T-shirt and no mascara.

But her mouth is red.

And she is surviving.

The light flickers again, and this time, I don't look away.

# Soundtrack of My Soul

I wish for a melody to cradle my days,
A symphony woven through life's shadowed, tangled maze.
For the laughter, the love, the sharp-stinging ache,
For mornings mundane and choices at stake.

Let joy be a crescendo, bold and bright,
A violin dancing in the morning light.
For sorrow, a haunting cello's deep moan,
Vibrating the silence, bone by bone.

Yet when the rhythm calls, I am set free,
Through beats that sway and taste like pure release.
Even in stillness, I twirl in my mind,
A dancer untethered, leaving worries behind.

I dance with joy, with pain, with grace,
Feet pounding the earth, a sacred embrace.
Even as tears blur the sight of my face,
The music spins me into a boundless space,
Where echoes fade and time cannot erase.

A harp to hum through the quietest hours,
Its notes like dew on the simplest of flowers.
And drums to thunder when passions ignite,
A primal pulse in the fading light.

Each note a chapter, each chord a refrain,
Weaving my story through sunshine and rain.
How sweet it would be to press "play" once more,
And relive the symphony I've sung before.

For every fragment, every fleeting phase,
There'd be music to match its silken, delicate haze.
A soundtrack of moments—both whispers and screams,
Composed to reflect a life full of dreams.

Perhaps this music lives within my core,
A silent score I've known forevermore.
Not needing instruments of wood and string,
But the vibrant hum that every moment brings.

# Outboard Engine

THE SUN'S LOW but still sharp, catching the edges of the old aluminum boat like a blade. He's hunched over the outboard engine, grease on his fingers, sweat darkening the back of his shirt. Tools are scattered in the grass. I'm holding a socket wrench, waiting for the next instruction.

It smells like oil and cut weeds and late afternoon.

He mutters to himself, trying to remember where he put the 9/16. Then he finds it behind the toolbox and laughs. "Losing my damn mind," he says, and I chuckle, because it's actually funny. Because in that moment, we're just two people trying to get something running.

No shouting. No silence. Just the easy rhythm of hands and tools and stories that come out sideways.

He tells me how he used to race boats when he was young. How he once outran a storm with a busted compass and pure guesswork. His eyes light up when he talks about it. He hands me a bolt to clean off with a rag and shows me the exact way to line up the grooves when it goes back in.

And I'm nodding, asking questions, not because I have to, but because I want to. Because I like this. I like him. Today.

And something shifts. Quietly. No thunder, no big reveal.

Just this small thought: What if I let that be enough?

Not forgiveness like forgetting. Not pretending nothing happened. Not rewriting the past.

But just… seeing him as he is right now.

A man with sunburned arms and a thousand regrets, who's never said sorry the way I wanted him to. Who still can't talk about feelings, but will talk for hours about carburetors. Who laughs when I get my hands dirty and says, "That's how you know you're doing it right."

I look at him—really look—and ask myself the only question that matters:

Do I like being here? With him? Today?

And the answer, surprisingly, is yes. I do.

Finally, after much tinkering and muttering, the engine caught. It sputtered, coughed out a plume of blue smoke that smelled acrid and familiar, then roared to life, the small aluminum boat vibrating beneath our feet. A wide, unrestrained beam spread across his face, making him look years younger. He clapped me on the shoulder, a solid, almost affectionate gesture. "See? Told you we could do it."

I smile, rag still in my hand, grease under my nails.

And I realized – for the first time, with a clarity that surprised me – I wasn't carrying him backward anymore, dragging the weight of the past into every interaction.

Just forward. From here.

In the simple act of working together, of sharing this small victory, that felt like the only way I knew how to truly begin to forgive.

# Its Brave to Ask for Help

Seeking help is a sign of strength,
not weakness.
Reach out to trusted people or professionals
when overwhelmed—
connection and support are vital parts of healing.

# Mosaic of Me

THE MIRROR SHATTERED, shards catching the dim light like a constellation of broken stars. Emily stared at her fragmented reflection, breath shallow. She had always been her harshest critic, but tonight, her self-doubt wasn't just whispering—it was screaming. The jagged pieces didn't just reflect her image; they threw back every insecurity, every unanswered question that had been quietly gnawing at her for years.

She dropped to the cold tile floor, her knees hitting hard, but she barely felt the pain. Tears streamed down her face, unchecked, hot against her skin. She wrapped her arms around herself in a fragile attempt to hold together the parts of her that felt like they were unraveling.

"Why can't I just be enough?" Her voice cracked in the silence, a brittle sound that echoed off the walls and came back empty.

She had been getting ready for a night out with Sarah, her closest friend since college. The outfit was flawless—the dress hugged her figure, the heels made her feel powerful—but the face in the mirror felt like a stranger's. She examined her features as if they were clues to a riddle she still hadn't solved: her dark, wavy hair that never seemed to cooperate, her deep brown eyes that always looked too intense, her olive-toned skin that reminded her of a lineage she couldn't fully grasp. Her full lips trembled.

None of it felt like her mother—the mother who had moved through the world like a painting come to life, all porcelain skin, blonde hair, and striking blue eyes. Emily loved her fiercely, but sometimes that love carried a weight. Looking in the mirror was like staring at a canvas painted in the wrong colors. "Whose face is this?" she whispered, as if the glass could answer. And when it didn't, the frustration surged. Her hand flew before she could stop herself, and the hairbrush smashed into the mirror, silencing the question with a crash.

Silence crept in, broken only by the soft drip of the faucet and the steady hum of the candle burning on the sink. Lavender hung in the air, sweet and mocking in its calm. It was meant to soothe her, but instead it felt like a reminder of all the peace she couldn't seem to find.

Then—three soft knocks. Emily flinched.

"Emily?" Sarah's voice floated through the door, gentle but laced with concern. "Are you okay?"

Emily hesitated. Her body screamed to hide, to say nothing, but her heart —exhausted and aching—longed to be seen. She cracked the door open.

"I'm fine," she said automatically, though her eyes betrayed the truth.

Sarah stepped inside, and in a heartbeat, her arms were around her. "Oh, Em…" Her voice broke a little as she took in the room—the shattered glass, the scent of lavender, the girl she loved like a sister, falling apart. "What happened?"

Emily clung to her, her sobs muffled against Sarah's shoulder. "I just… I'm so tired of pretending. Of trying to be someone I don't recognize."

"You don't have to pretend. Not with me." Sarah's voice was low and certain. "You're not alone in this."

They sank to the floor together, surrounded by fragments of silvered glass and unspoken feelings. Sarah reached for Emily's hand, grounding her.

"Remember that art exhibit we went to?" she said softly, brushing Emily's hair back. "The one that had all the mirrors?"

Emily nodded, a shaky breath escaping her lips. "Yeah."

"There was that one piece—remember? It showed how mirrors reflect different versions of us depending on the angle, the lighting, the distance." She smiled gently. "You said it made you feel seen."

Emily nodded again, slower this time. "It was beautiful."

"That's how I see you. You're not broken. You're layered. Complex. Beautiful in ways you haven't even discovered yet. Just because you don't always recognize what you see doesn't mean it's not still you."

Something cracked open inside Emily—not like the mirror, but like light breaking through a clouded sky. Her grip on Sarah's hand tightened.

"Thank you," she said, her voice barely audible. "I think… I think I needed someone to remind me I'm allowed to be a work in progress."

Sarah smiled. "We all are. Let's clean this up, make some tea, and just sit. You don't have to say anything else if you don't want to."

And as they picked up the shards, piece by piece, Emily felt the faintest flicker of something returning to her—something like grace. Not everything could be fixed tonight. But maybe, just maybe, she was starting to believe that healing didn't have to be perfect. It just had to begin.

About a week earlier, Emily had been digging through boxes in the attic of her childhood home—chasing some vague sense of nostalgia, maybe, or just trying to feel closer to something real. Among the old yearbooks and faded photo albums, she found a dusty, leather-bound journal. It was tucked away in the corner, nearly forgotten, its spine weathered and soft with time. Something about it felt sacred.

227

Curious, Emily opened the worn cover and began to read. Her breath caught as she realized it belonged to her mother—Margaret. Each page was filled with careful, looping script that she recognized from childhood birthday cards and notes in lunchboxes. But these weren't the polished words of a mother writing to her child. These were raw, private entries— confessions written to no one, full of emotion and vulnerability. And then one entry stopped her cold.

June 15, 1995
I don't know how to put this into words, but I need to get it out. Robert and I have decided to keep this a secret, but it's weighing heavily on me. Emily is not our biological daughter. We adopted her when she was just a baby. Her birth mother, Selena, was my best friend. We were both pregnant at the same time, sharing our hopes and dreams for our children. But then, tragedy struck.

Emily's hands began to shake. The words blurred on the page as she read them again, as if repetition could soften their impact. Her heart pounded in her chest—part disbelief, part recognition. Deep down, a small voice whispered that this made sense. She had always felt it. A quiet dissonance. Like a note that never quite belonged in the melody of her family.

Desperate for more, she flipped through the pages, landing on the next entry.

July 2, 1995
Selena and I were so excited about our pregnancies. We'd stay up late, dreaming about playdates and matching Halloween costumes. But I went into labor too early. The doctors tried everything, but our baby didn't survive. The grief was unbearable. Robert and I felt like our world had collapsed.

Emily pressed her hand to her chest, aching for a woman who had lived with that kind of loss—and who had somehow still found room to love again.

*July 10, 1995*
*A week later, Selena went into labor. It was supposed to be a celebration. But there were complications. She died giving birth... leaving behind her daughter. We made the decision that day. Robert and I would raise her as our own. We named her Emily, after my grandmother. She brought light into our darkness.*

By now, tears rolled freely down Emily's cheeks. The grief, the love, the impossible choices—they wove a picture she had never imagined. She felt a deep sorrow for Selena, the mother she had never known. And overwhelming gratitude for Margaret and Robert, who had taken a devastating loss and turned it into love.

*August 15, 1995*
*Raising Emily has been the greatest gift. But I live with the fear that one day, she'll find out the truth. Will she still see me as her mother? Will she feel like she belongs? I hope she knows that she is— completely, wholly—our daughter.*

Tucked between the pages, a photo slipped out and fluttered into her lap. It was Emily as a child, no older than six. Her eyes sparkled with that wide-open wonder only children have. She looked happy. Untouched by questions of identity or belonging. Emily stared at it, her throat tight, realizing how long it had been since she felt that free in her own skin.

She closed the journal slowly, like sealing away something sacred again— but different now. The truth didn't shatter her. In a strange way, it clarified her. The years of feeling like she didn't quite fit, the endless striving to prove she was enough—it all made sense now. Her fears weren't just about beauty or expectations. They were about belonging.

Later that evening, she sat with Sarah on the couch, dressed in the outfit they'd picked out earlier, but with nowhere to go. The night out had quietly transformed into something else entirely—something quieter and far more meaningful. They sipped tea, the silence between them full of understanding.

Emily told her everything.

And when she finished, Sarah reached across and squeezed her hand. "You don't have to carry this alone," she said softly.

"I know," Emily replied, her voice steadier than it had been in days. "But I think this next part... I need to do it by myself."

She shared her plan to visit her childhood home the next morning. Not just to retrace her steps, but to reconnect with the girl in that photograph. The girl who didn't know about loss or lineage or complicated truths. The girl who loved herself, fully and without apology.

Sarah nodded. "I'll be here when you get back."

And for the first time in a long time, Emily believed she might actually come back a little more whole.

As Emily walked through the familiar streets of her childhood neighborhood, a quiet nostalgia settled over her like a warm breeze. Every corner held a memory—the park where she learned to ride her bike, the sidewalks where she'd raced her sister barefoot in the summer, the towering oak trees that had watched her grow. The scent of freshly cut grass lingered in the air, mixing with the distant sound of children's laughter. It was like stepping into a living photograph—one slightly faded, but still full of life.

She turned the corner and saw it—her old house. The white picket fence was still standing, though the paint had chipped with age. Rose bushes bloomed wildly along the front path, their petals soft and unruly, like time had allowed nature to reclaim a bit of the order. The windows, once so familiar, now seemed to hold their own quiet secrets.

She paused at the gate, her heartbeat loud in her ears. Then, with a breath, she walked up the steps and knocked.

An elderly woman answered, her face kind and open. "Can I help you?" she asked gently, her voice tinged with warmth.

"Hi… I'm Emily. I grew up here. I was wondering if… if I could come in for a moment. Just to look around."

The woman studied her for a second, then smiled. "Of course, dear. Come on in. I always love hearing stories about this place."

As Emily stepped inside, the air welcomed her like an old friend. The floorboards creaked beneath her feet—the same creak in the same spots —and the scent of lavender and aged wood filled the hallway. Her fingers traced the curve of the banister, its familiar grooves a map of her childhood. The wallpaper, faded now, still carried the same delicate floral pattern, worn but not forgotten.

In the living room, an old clock ticked softly, each beat echoing through the silence. A radio played in the background, its tune slow and hauntingly familiar, like something her mother used to hum. The room seemed unchanged, yet quieter—like it had been holding its breath, waiting for her to return.

Then she stepped into the dining room, and a memory struck her like a gust of wind.

She was eight years old again, sitting at the long wooden table with her family. Her younger sister, Lily, had looked at her with innocent curiosity.

"Emily, why don't you look like the rest of us?" Lily asked, her wide eyes unfiltered by malice—just honest wonder. "Your hair is darker. And your skin, your eyes… they're different."

At the time, Emily hadn't known what to say. She turned to her parents, searching for reassurance. But what she saw instead was a quick glance exchanged between them—tight, uneasy.

231

"Everyone's unique, sweetheart," Margaret had said, her voice too controlled, too careful. "Emily is special, just like you."

But even at eight, Emily had caught the tension. The way her father busied himself with his fork, the way no one met her eyes.

That was the first time she truly felt like she didn't belong.

She remembered the comments over the years—how people in town would ask where she got her hair, how some assumed she was part Latina and tried to speak Spanish to her. Her parents would brush it off, saying she took after an obscure great-aunt or her father's "Mediterranean roots." The answers never satisfied her. They never felt like the truth. And now, she finally knew why.

The next morning, Emily made her way to her grandmother Evelyn's cottage. The garden was in full bloom, wildflowers swaying in the breeze, bees lazily buzzing from bloom to bloom. They sat in the shade, sunlight dappling through the leaves.

As Emily poured out her heart—the journal, the truth, the ache of it all— Evelyn listened quietly. Not once did she interrupt. When Emily finished, Evelyn reached over and took her hand.

"Your mother told me everything, years ago," she said softly. "She made me promise never to say a word, unless you asked. We wanted to protect you. But I understand now—maybe silence can hurt more than the truth."

Emily looked down, wiping her eyes. "I feel like I don't know who I am anymore."

Evelyn reached into her pocket and pulled out a small, worn photograph. "This is Selena—your birth mother. She was about your age here."

Emily took the photo with trembling hands. The resemblance was undeniable—same rich, dark hair, same deep brown eyes that seemed to carry entire stories within them. Her breath caught.

"She named you Maria Elena," Evelyn said gently. "But your mother—Margaret—thought calling you Emily would help you fit in here. She wanted to protect you in the only way she knew how. She never meant to erase your identity. But I know… sometimes love tries so hard to protect, it forgets that the truth matters too."

Emily nodded slowly, the photograph pressed to her chest. "I get it now. I really do. I just… I wish I had known sooner. Maybe I wouldn't have spent so much time trying to be someone I'm not."

"You were never pretending," Evelyn said firmly. "You were becoming. You're still becoming."

She gave Emily's hand a reassuring squeeze. "You are Emily. But you're also Maria Elena. You carry both names, both stories. And that's not a contradiction—it's a gift. You're not lost. You're layered."

Emily let the words sink in. For the first time in a long time, they didn't land as pressure to figure it all out—but as permission to take her time. To hold both grief and gratitude. To let healing be slow.

She looked back down at the photo, the edges soft with time, and smiled through her tears.

Maybe, just maybe, she was finally beginning to see herself clearly—not in a mirror, but in the lineage of love that had shaped her, however complicated, however imperfect.

With her grandmother's words echoing in her heart, Emily began the quiet, deliberate work of rebuilding herself—not into someone new, but into someone more fully seen. Therapy became a refuge, a space where she could begin to unravel the tangled threads of insecurity with compassion instead of shame. Journaling followed, each page a gentle exhale. As she wrote, she uncovered not just pain, but clarity. Her worth, she realized, had never been rooted in biology or appearance. It lived in the love she gave, the kindness she carried, the resilience etched into her bones.

Slowly, she stopped seeing herself as a cracked mirror and started seeing herself as a mosaic—beautiful not despite the pieces, but because of them.

Longing to understand where she truly came from, Emily set off on a transformative journey to Mexico. It wasn't just a trip—it was a pilgrimage to a past she'd never known but always felt. As she wandered through vibrant markets brimming with color and life, the air filled with the scent of sizzling tortillas and ripe fruit, something in her shifted. The streets pulsed with music—mariachi horns blaring from street corners, laughter rising like wind through palm leaves. It felt less like discovering a new place and more like meeting a part of herself for the first time.

One mural, in particular, stopped her in her tracks. It stretched across a sun-soaked wall, a riot of color and symbolism. At the center stood a woman tall and proud, her arms open wide as if embracing the whole community. Her eyes glinted with quiet determination, her hair braided with marigolds that shimmered gold in the afternoon light. Around her, generations of people—grandparents, children, workers, artists—stood together, hands linked, hearts unified. It was strength. It was belonging. It was hope.

Emily stepped closer, her breath caught in her throat. She felt something stir deep within—recognition. Not of the woman, but of the feeling. The sense of coming home to herself.

Moved, she pulled out her phone and captured the mural. As she did, she noticed a man on a ladder adding final brushstrokes to the bottom corner.

"Excuse me," she called, her voice soft but sure. "Are you the artist?"

The man climbed down, wiping his hands. "Yes, I am," he replied with a warm smile. "My name's Diego."

"It's beautiful," Emily said. "The woman in the mural… she feels so strong, like she's holding everyone together."

Diego nodded thoughtfully. "She is. She's inspired by my grandmother. She was the heart of our family—resilient, nurturing, endlessly hopeful. I painted her to honor all the women who carry generations on their shoulders."

Emily swallowed hard, emotion thick in her throat. "She reminds me of someone too. And of myself, in a way. I've been on a journey… trying to find the parts of me that got lost or hidden. Your mural—it brought something forward I didn't know I needed."

Diego's eyes softened. "That's why I paint. Art tells the stories we don't always know how to speak. It reminds us we're part of something bigger —history, community, legacy. Sometimes it even helps us find our way back to ourselves."

They stood in silence for a moment, sharing a quiet understanding. Then Emily smiled. "Thank you, Diego. This… it means more than I can say."

"I'm glad," he replied, his voice gentle. "This wall may hold my grandmother's spirit, but now it holds yours too."

As Emily continued exploring the city, she found herself drawn to mural after mural—each one a thread in the larger tapestry of the culture she was rediscovering. One burst with energy, portraying a bustling mercado alive with color and movement: vendors bartering, children darting between stalls, and elders laughing beneath woven canopies. It sang of community and the everyday beauty of tradition.

Another mural depicted a group of women weaving intricate textiles, their hands steady, their expressions serene. The layers of fabric they created mirrored the layers of history, memory, and care passed down through generations. Emily stood in awe of their grace and the quiet strength in their work.

Still another showed revolutionaries mid-battle, their eyes ablaze with defiance, their fists raised in resistance. The bold strokes and fiery colors captured a spirit of rebellion and the relentless pursuit of freedom. Emily felt the power of that struggle, and how it echoed her own—different, but rooted in the same desire to claim identity and agency.

With every mural, Emily gathered pieces of herself she hadn't known were missing. The culture, the stories, the legacy of resilience—it all wove itself into her. These weren't just beautiful paintings. They were mirrors, too. Not of how she looked, but of who she was and who she was becoming.

On one of her last nights in Mexico, Emily found herself sitting alone in a sun-drenched plaza, the air thick with the golden glow of sunset and the rhythmic pulse of a live band playing traditional Mexican music. Laughter danced through the warm breeze, mixing with the scent of grilled corn and blooming jasmine. Couples twirled under strings of glowing lights, their bodies moving in perfect harmony with the music—fluid, joyful, free.

Emily sat at the edge of it all, a quiet observer, her heart full yet still searching for something she couldn't quite name.

A man approached her, his presence calm and confident, with a smile that felt like an invitation.

"Would you like to dance?" he asked, offering his hand.

She hesitated, her old voice whispering doubts—What if I mess up? What if I don't belong here either? But when she looked into his eyes, something shifted. There was no judgment, only kindness. And maybe, for the first time, she felt ready to stop asking for permission to be here.

She smiled and took his hand. "I'd love to."

He introduced himself as Javier and gently guided her to the center of the plaza. "It's salsa," he explained with a wink. "But I'll take it slow."

As the music swelled, he led her through the steps with patient ease. The rhythm found its way into her body, loosening her limbs and quieting her mind. With every turn and dip, something inside her uncoiled. Her laughter came freely, her movements light, as if the music itself had peeled away the last of her fear.

"You're a natural," Javier said, his voice warm.

Emily laughed. "I think you're just a good teacher."

"Maybe," he said, "but it's you who's dancing."

In that moment, spinning under the soft lights with the plaza alive around her, Emily felt something she hadn't felt in years—free. She wasn't hiding. She wasn't shrinking. She was present, open, alive.

So this is what it feels like to let go, she thought. To connect. To trust.

Dancing with Javier didn't just teach her about movement—it taught her about vulnerability, about what it means to lean in and let someone else guide without losing yourself. She didn't have to be perfect to be worthy of the moment. She just had to be here.

And perhaps, that was the most profound part of all.

She carried that feeling with her in the days and weeks that followed—walking the city's streets one last time, her senses tuned to every brushstroke of culture, every echo of resilience.

The murals she passed—marketplaces alive with barter, women weaving centuries of heritage into fabric, revolutionaries with fire in their eyes—seemed to speak directly to her now. They reminded her that identity is not a single thread, but a tapestry of inherited strength and chosen paths.

She didn't need to know all the answers. She just had to keep listening. Keep showing up.

---

Back home, months later, Emily stood before a mirror in her apartment. This one was whole. Clean lines, no cracks. But she didn't need the mirror to see herself clearly anymore.

She looked at her reflection—not for flaws, but for truth.

She saw a woman who had faced her shadows and walked through them. Who had held grief in one hand and love in the other. Who had danced with fear and come out stronger. She saw someone worthy.

Someone enough.

A buzz from her phone broke the silence. A message from Sarah: "Hey, want to grab coffee later?"
Emily smiled and replied, "Absolutely."

As she set the phone down, her eyes returned to the mirror. Around the frame, a collage of photos had begun to grow—a quiet gallery of her mosaic life.

There was one of her biological mother, Selena, her eyes shimmering with quiet pride. Next to it, a photo of Margaret—her adoptive mother—with that steady, safe smile that had comforted her for so long.
Beside them, a snapshot of the mural in Mexico—the woman with marigolds in her hair, arms outstretched, standing tall amidst her people. And tucked beside that, a candid photo from the plaza: Emily and Javier mid-dance, her eyes lit up with unfiltered joy, his hand gently guiding her in the blur of music and lights.

Each photo held a piece of her story. Not perfect, not polished—but real. Raw. Whole.

She stepped back, took it all in, and let herself smile. These weren't just memories. They were proof. That she had loved. That she had grown. That she had returned to herself.

She knew there would still be hard days. Questions without answers. Moments of doubt. But now she had something she hadn't before—an anchor. A truth she could return to again and again:

She didn't need to be more.
She didn't need to be different.
She was enough.

Just as she was.

# Be Present with Yourself

Mindfulness isn't just meditation—
it's slowing down, noticing your thoughts,
and reconnecting with the moment.
Start with a few deep breaths
and let yourself be without judgment.

# The Light One

WE'RE SITTING ON her porch, drinking something warm even though it's hot out. She's laughing about a guy she's seeing—another one with too many tattoos and not enough ambition.

And I want to roll my eyes, like I always do.
I want to say, You never learn,
but I don't.

She's barefoot, legs up on the table, like she's still sixteen and hasn't broken anything that matters, spooning Nutella straight from the jar with the back of a pen, with hands that never learned how to hold consequences.

She grins when she sees me watching, like a kid caught red-handed but never punished. "I couldn't find a spoon," she shrugs, not remotely sorry. She never seems to care about the mess she leaves, about the things she doesn't clean up, about the way she takes up space without ever asking for permission.

And for a moment, I feel that same old knot twist in my chest.

The one made of all the years I played the role she never had to.
The steady one.
The fixer.
The one who paid bills on time and stayed when things got hard and swallowed the hard truth that love in our family was given in conditions, not warmth.

241

She used to cry and they'd hold her.
I used to cry and they'd say, You're stronger than that.
She failed and they sighed.
I stumbled and they looked disappointed, like I'd let the whole world
down.

She was the light one.
The float.
I was the weight.

And I've carried that weight for so long—
not just mine, but theirs, and hers too.

She says something then, about Mom always making her favorite meal
and how she thought it was funny that she never had to ask.
I almost say, Yeah, you never had to ask for anything,
but something in me softens.

Because I look at her and see it—
that same tired under her eyes.
That quiet ache of someone who's been told she's not made for carrying,
so she never learned how to stand alone.

I used to envy the way they never expected anything from her.
But now, sitting across from her in the fading light,
I realize how lonely that must've been too.
To be everyone's baby, forever.
To never be trusted with the hard stuff.
To be praised for breathing, but never believed in.

She's not the reason they loved me differently.

She's not the weight.

And maybe the only way I get free is by setting her down—
not from blame, but from expectation.
Not from distance, but from resentment.

I reach across the table.
Touch her hand.
She looks up, surprised.
And I say, "You know… I'm glad you're happy right now."

She smiles, small and honest.

And in that quiet, I feel it—
not a grand revelation, not some sweeping forgiveness.
Just the gentle loosening of a grip I've held too tight for too long.

I don't need to keep score anymore.

I just want to love her.

Because that, finally, feels like freedom.

# *Two Steps Back*

To step back is not to lose—
it's to listen to the quiet voice
that says: *not yet, not this way, not now.*

It's leaving the well-worn path
to walk through uncertainty alone,
bracing against the wind
that asks, *Are you sure?*

It's planting seeds no one will see,
trusting in something underground,
invisible, unhurried—
work that won't be witnessed,
work that won't be praised.

The world will call you foolish.
"Too slow," they'll say, turning away.
But they can't see beneath the surface,
where roots are forming,
where fire is being forged.

To step back is to close a door
on what you thought you needed—
the job, the lover, the version of yourself
that fit so neatly into other people's plans.

Some losses clear the way
for something truer to take root.
Some goodbyes are the price
of finally becoming free.

To retreat is not to surrender—
it's to gather strength,
to breathe before the next push,
to pull back like an archer
so the arrow can fly farther.

Two steps back,
not defeat—
just preparation.

Think of the artist who quit the steady job
to paint in a cramped studio,
brushes still wrapped,
rent unpaid,
but finally, *finally*, making something real.

Think of the dreamer sleeping under stars,
building a kingdom no one else can see yet,
dismissed as crazy, reckless, lost—
but certain of the vision only they can hold.

Think of the mother working night shifts,
pouring herself into exhaustion,
so her children can stand in sunlight
she may never feel on her own skin.

Or the one who walks away from the crowd,
who listens to the dream no one else hears,
who risks being misunderstood
because the cost of staying small
is higher than the cost of leaping.

The tension before the leap—
that's where transformation lives.

Yes, be foolish.
Be reckless.
Be the kind of crazy that builds cathedrals,
writes symphonies,
changes the world.

Because every star in the sky
seemed impossible once.

The edge is waiting.
The leap is coming.
But first—
the step back.
The rooted deep.
The gathering of all you are
before you fly.

To lose is not the end.
To lose is to learn what matters.
To strip away what doesn't serve you
and discover what remains.

Through silence,
through shadows,
through the doubt that whispers you *can't*—
the brave keep moving.

Two steps back,
then the leap.

Not retreat.
Preparation.

Not failure.
Flight.

# Second Mug

THE KITCHEN IS still. Morning spills in through the blinds in soft, slanted stripes. I pad across the tile in thick socks, the ones with the frayed heel, and reach for the coffee canister like I do everyday.

Scoop. Pour. Button.

The machine groans to life.

I open the cupboard and pull down two mugs without thinking—one plain white, the other chipped at the rim, navy with a faded constellation print. The kind that used to prompt a story. The kind that always ended in a laugh.

My hand pauses.

I should put one back. I don't need two anymore. Haven't for months.

I hover, unsure.

But something in me resists the motion. I set both mugs down on the counter.

The coffee drips, slow and steady, the smell curling into the air like memory.

When it's ready, I fill them both.

I carry them to the kitchen table and sit, wrapping my hands around the plain one. The other mug sits across from me, untouched, steam rising soft and ghostlike above it.

I don't pretend he's here.

I don't say anything out loud.

But I let the second mug stay full.

And for once, the silence doesn't feel like absence.

It just feels… still.

It just feels like morning.

And in that quiet, I feel something settle back into place..

you are allowed to miss
who you were,
even as you honor
who you are becoming

# Two Inches of Rain

THE STORM HAS been coming all day.

You could feel it in the weight of the air, the way the birds went silent, the way the world held its breath. Now it's here, and I'm standing in it—barefoot in the backyard, in the mud, in what used to be a garden.

Water runs down my arms and into my sleeves. It slips between the collar of my old hoodie and my skin like a cold secret. My breath fogs in the air, even though it's warm. I haven't spoken to anyone today. Not since the email. Not since the last number turned red and everything tipped over.

Two inches of rain.

That's what the forecast said. As if grief can be measured like that. Two inches. Just enough to ruin the soil. Just enough to drown the sprouts I planted last week when I still believed in "starting over."

My toes sink into the earth. The ground is soft, messy. I don't even know why I came out here.

I guess I needed to see the damage with my own eyes.

Lightning flickers like a flashbulb, quick and jagged. I blink into the dark, and that's when I see it.

A sprout.

Tiny. Green. Brave. Pushing up through the muck like it doesn't care that the sky is falling. Just two leaves, trembling.

I crouch beside it, my knees sinking into the wet ground. I don't touch it. I just watch. Raindrops hit the earth around it like applause.

It shouldn't have made it.

But here it is.

And suddenly, I'm not thinking about the email. Or the job. Or the fact that my life doesn't look anything like I thought it would.

I'm thinking about that sprout.

How it decided to live anyway.

How maybe… I can too.

# Own Your Hard

Knuckles white, you hold on tight—
every breath a fight through endless night.
Staying costs you everything you are.
But letting go? That leaves a deeper scar.

The rope is fraying in your hands.
You hear it whisper: shift your plans.
But what waits below, you cannot see,
and falling feels worse than never being free.

It's hard to hold on.
It's hard to let go.

Two kinds of pain, both sharp and real—
the ache of chains, or wounds that will not heal.
The weight of staying where you've always been,
or stepping out and starting over again.

Neither path will spare you from the cost.
Neither saves you from what's loved or lost.

But here's the truth you need to know:
You have to choose which way to go.

Not because one's right, the other wrong.
Not because there's somewhere you belong
where pain won't find you, won't take hold—
but staying stuck will leave you frozen cold.

So choose the hard that sets you free.
Choose the hard that lets you finally be
the person waiting on the other side,
not the one who stayed because they're terrified.

Your pain is yours.
Your hard is yours.
And so is your life—
once you stop searching for easier doors
and walk the path that's true,
the one that leads you back to you.

# While I Bled

THEY TALKED TO my pain like it was the problem.

Like the bleeding was a choice I was making, a mood I could shift, a perspective that needed adjusting. They had so much to say about how I was handling it—my tone, my timing, my failure to suffer more quietly. They were very concerned about my pain. How it made them uncomfortable. How it was inconvenient. How maybe if I just thought about it differently, breathed more deeply, tried harder, wanted it less, the pain would simply evaporate and we could all move on.

Meanwhile, I was bleeding.

Not metaphorically. Not in some abstract, poetic sense. There was a wound. It had a source. It was actively happening. And they were standing there with their advice and their suggestions and their thinly veiled annoyance, talking to the symptoms while refusing to acknowledge the cause.

"Have you tried being more positive?"

I'm bleeding.

"You need to take responsibility for your healing."

I'm still bleeding.

"Some people have it worse, you know."

I know. And I'm bleeding.

This is what it feels like to suffer in front of people who can't or won't see the wound. Who mistake your pain for a personality defect. Who think that if they just say the right thing, use the right tone, give you the right advice, you'll stop bleeding all over their nice clean floor and they can get back to pretending everything is fine.

They don't want to know about the wound. The wound is complicated. The wound might implicate them or require them to feel something uncomfortable or demand that they do something other than dispense wisdom from a safe distance. The wound might be ongoing, might not have an easy solution, might require sustained attention and care and actual change.

So they talk to the pain instead. Because pain is your problem. Pain is something wrong with you. Pain is something you're doing, or not doing, or doing wrong. Pain is manageable if they can just convince you to manage it better.

But the wound? The wound is still there. Still open. Still bleeding.

I had a parent who talked to my anxiety without ever addressing the chaos they created in the house. They had a lot to say about how I needed to calm down, relax, stop being so sensitive. They never once looked at the yelling, the unpredictability, the walking on eggshells, the environment that made anxiety the only rational response. They treated my fear like a defect in my manufacturing rather than an adaptation to my circumstances.

I bled. They talked to my bleeding. They never touched the knife.

I had a partner who talked to my anger without ever acknowledging what kept making me angry. They wanted me to be less reactive, more understanding, willing to let things go. They had workshops to recommend, books I should read, techniques I should try. What they didn't have was any willingness to stop doing the thing that was hurting me. My anger was the problem. Their behavior was just "who they were" and I needed to accept it.

I bled. They critiqued my bleeding. They never removed the blade.

I had friends who talked to my depression without ever asking why I was depressed. They sent me articles about exercise and sunlight and gratitude practices. They told me about their cousin who tried this supplement or their coworker who did that meditation. They meant well, I think. But meaning well while ignoring the wound is its own kind of violence.

Because here's what they couldn't or wouldn't see: I wasn't depressed in a vacuum. I was depressed because I was exhausted from pretending to be fine. Because I was isolated. Because I was giving more than I had to people who took without thinking. Because the structures of my life were grinding me down and everyone wanted me to adjust my attitude about the grinding instead of questioning why I was being ground in the first place.

I bled. They offered band-aids for a severed artery. They never asked who was holding the saw.

This is the loneliness of being wounded in a world that only wants to talk about your pain. They'll discuss your symptoms endlessly. Your crying is too much. Your silence is concerning. Your anger is inappropriate. Your sadness is a downer. Your fear is irrational. Your pain is inconvenient.

But the thing causing the pain? That's off limits. That's too complicated. That's not their responsibility. That's just life, just the way things are, just something you need to learn to cope with better.

257

So you learn to be wounded quietly. You learn to bleed in private. You learn to show up with the blood cleaned off, the pain managed, the wound covered, so that people can be comfortable around you. You learn that your survival depends on making your suffering invisible, because visible suffering makes people uncomfortable, and their comfort matters more than your healing.

You learn to say "I'm fine" when you're hemorrhaging. You learn to apologize for bleeding on people who stabbed you. You learn to thank people for their advice about your pain while they ignore the knife in your back that they're standing on to get a better view.

And the worst part—the part that makes you question your own reality—is that they're so convinced they're helping. They genuinely believe that if they just give you enough strategies for managing pain, enough tips for staying positive, enough reminders that other people have it worse, you'll stop making such a fuss and get over it already.

They don't understand that you can't think your way out of a wound. You can't meditate away a knife. You can't gratitude-journal yourself into not bleeding when something is actively cutting you.

But they need to believe you can. Because if your pain isn't just a matter of perspective, if it's actually a response to real harm, then someone is responsible for that harm. Maybe them. Maybe a system they benefit from. Maybe a situation they don't want to change because changing it would cost them something.

So they talk to your pain. They pathologize your response to injury. They make the bleeding your fault, your choice, your failure to cope. Because that's easier than acknowledging the wound. Easier than doing something about it. Easier than admitting they might be part of what's hurting you.

I had therapists who wanted to treat my symptoms without addressing my circumstances. Who had diagnoses and medications and coping strategies but no analysis of the situations I was coping with. Who wanted me to be more resilient to abuse instead of questioning why I was expected to be resilient to it in the first place.

I bled. They taught me breathing exercises. They never questioned what was taking my breath away.

I had employers who wanted to address my burnout without addressing my workload. Who offered wellness programs and mindfulness apps and pizza parties while piling more work on fewer people. Who wanted me to be more efficient, more positive, more grateful for the opportunity to slowly destroy myself for their profit.

I bled. They gave me a ping-pong table. They never reduced the bleeding.

I had a society that wanted to talk about mental health while ignoring economic violence, systemic oppression, the grinding poverty and precarity that creates mental health crises in the first place. That wanted me to work on my individual healing while refusing to address collective harm.

I bled. They told me to practice self-care. They never stopped the cutting.

And I tried. God, I tried. I did the breathing exercises and the gratitude journals and the positive thinking and the meditation and the therapy and the medication and all the things you're supposed to do to manage pain in a world that creates it constantly and then blames you for hurting.

But you know what I learned? You can't heal a wound that's still being inflicted. You can't recover from harm that's ongoing. You can't build resilience to a knife that's still in your back.

At some point, someone has to address the wound. Someone has to remove the blade. Someone has to stop the active harm and give the injury a chance to close.

But that would require people to look at the wound. To acknowledge it. To take responsibility for it, or at least stop pretending it doesn't exist. It would require them to do something other than talk to your pain like your pain is the problem.

So what do you do when people refuse to see your wound? When they insist on treating your bleeding as a behavioral issue, a perspective problem, a failure of resilience?

You stop expecting them to understand. You stop trying to make them see what they're determined not to see. You stop bleeding for an audience that critiques your bleeding instead of helping you stop.

And you find the people who see wounds. Who don't flinch from them. Who don't immediately start offering advice about pain management when you show them you're hurt. Who ask "what happened?" instead of "have you tried yoga?" Who understand that healing requires addressing causes, not just managing symptoms.

You find the people who look at your bleeding and say: "That needs stitches. That needs care. That needs to stop happening to you."

You find the people who are willing to help you remove the knife instead of teaching you to be more comfortable with it lodged in your spine.

You find the people who understand that sometimes the most compassionate thing isn't advice about pain—it's witness to the wound. It's validation that the wound is real, that it hurts, that it shouldn't be happening, that your pain is a reasonable response to injury, not a character flaw or a coping deficit.

You find the people who don't need you to bleed quietly. Who don't require you to package your suffering in ways that make them comfortable. Who can sit with your pain without needing to fix it, explain it, or minimize it.

And with those people, something strange happens: the bleeding slows. Not because they gave you better advice about managing pain, but because they helped you address the wound. Because they saw you. Because they believed you. Because they didn't make you prove that the knife was real before they'd help you remove it.

This is what healing actually looks like. Not positive thinking while you bleed. Not resilience to ongoing harm. Not learning to cope better with what shouldn't be happening to you in the first place.

But the removal of the blade. The cleaning of the wound. The space to recover without someone standing over you asking when you'll be done healing already.

The people who talk to your pain while you bleed will never understand this. They'll keep offering their advice, their strategies, their suggestions for managing what they refuse to see. They'll keep treating your symptoms while ignoring your wound.

Let them.

You don't need them to understand anymore. You don't need their validation or their advice or their comfort. You just need them to get out of the way so you can find the people who actually know how to help.

The people who see the wound.

The people who stop the bleeding.

The people who understand that sometimes
the most revolutionary act
isn't learning to cope with the knife
—it's pulling it out.

# Acknowledge How Far You've Come.

Progress isn't always visible,
but it's always worth celebrating.
Reflect on your journey—
every small step forward matters.
You're growing,
even on the hard days.

# *Will You Dance With Me?*

When life gives you a moment, a blink in the blur,
To stand still or move—be bold, choose the stir.
When the world says "wait," or "maybe just glance,"
You look it straight on and say, "No, I'll dance!"

Not hidden in shadows, not lost in the crowd,
But fully alive, raw, real, and proud.
Forget flawless timing or knowing the song,
This isn't about right—it's about being strong.

Because dancing, my friend, isn't steps on the floor,
It's a heartbeat unleashed, it's a soul wanting more.
It's laughter through tears, it's chaos and grace,
It's finding your light in a dark, crowded place.

So dance when you're aching, dance when you're free,
Dance when you're broken, whoever you be.
The world may be watching—but let them all see
That joy is defiant, and it starts with me.

Today I found rhythm in the rush of the day,
A flicker of beauty that wouldn't just stay.
So I grabbed it, I held it, I let my soul soar,
And I danced like I never had danced before.

Now I'm reaching for you with an open, brave hand—
Not to lead, not to teach, just to help you to stand.
Because maybe together, just maybe, we'll find
That courage and dancing were always entwined.

Will you rise from your corner, your silence, your trance?
Will you say yes to joy? Will you take a chance?
I'm not asking for perfect—I just want to see
You move in your truth...

Will you dance with me?

# Roots, Not Ruins

WHAT IS LIFE, when your only options are boiling water or hot oil?

Apparently, it's called growth—at least according to self-help blogs written by people with stable upbringings and trust funds.

I was freshly 21 when I met him, but I might as well have been 16—emotionally, spiritually, maybe even biologically stunted by a life spent marinating in small-town dysfunction. He was 40. Sophisticated. Experienced. Well-traveled. Basically, a walking red flag wearing cologne that cost more than my monthly food budget.

When you escape the pot of boiling water only to swan dive into the deep fryer, you don't immediately feel the burn. It's warm, even comforting. That's how my escape from a lifetime of abuse felt. The illusion of choice made it feel like a victory. Freedom, even if it meant stepping directly into another cage—as long as this one had Wi-Fi and matching curtains.

He wasn't particularly handsome. He wasn't rich. He didn't even say the right things. But desperation has a way of polishing turds into potential. I imagined this choice would unlock the glamorous montage of healing and personal growth—traveling, learning, loving. I'd envisioned doing all those things solo, but we all have to start somewhere, right? Even if that somewhere is a tiny city apartment with a man who thought "emotional availability" was a cocktail.

Still, he encouraged me to chase my Architecture degree, noting that I'd never lost my passion or talent for it. Sweet, right? Almost like he cared.

**Almost.** But pursuing that dream meant moving to the city and moving in with him. And after a year of battling through irrelevant coursework and creeping existential dread, I dropped out. Not just of school, but of the version of my life that I thought I was building. And now I was far from home, without a degree, low-key codependent, and barely surviving the city's pace—like a turtle with a MetroCard.

The manipulation was subtle at first, masked as helpful critiques and love-laced suggestions. He loved Jay-Z, which was fine until Beyoncé dropped "Upgrade U," and suddenly I was his DIY project. He told me I dressed "too simple and comfortably"—the way one might describe a couch cover at a retirement home. He said it made him cringe to be seen with me in public. I needed to carry a giant, empty purse (because aesthetics), and my hair—naturally sun-kissed to a soft gold every summer—was apparently too close to my skin tone. "It makes you look dusty," he said. Dusty. Like I was an old photo album in someone else's attic.

No alarms went off. I was being **upgraded.** I took it all in stride—except for the cringe comment. That one broke something. I remember taking a midday shower just to cry in silence. Soap can't wash off that kind of insult, but I gave it a go anyway.

So there I was: faithless, lost, and performing the role of "ambitious student" to anyone who asked. I smiled bright enough to burn retinas when I talked about my Architecture degree. I got wined and dined at places where the bread came with edible flowers and the waiters judged you silently for asking what they were. I met influencers and industry elites, had regular nail and hair appointments—because "the look" mattered more than how dead you felt inside.

I hated every second of it. The fake laughter, the fake people, the Botoxed conversations that felt like reading cue cards from a reality show. And the night always ended with us talking about how vapid they all were, critiquing their clothes, their careers, their laugh lines. Turns out, I was becoming exactly what I hated—a well-dressed hater. I didn't even notice when I became fluent in Gossip and got my Mean Girl passport stamped. Regina George would be proud of this shallow, judgmental cliché she could weaponize without lifting a manicured finger.

And somehow, I told myself, this was what living must feel like.

What had I become?

The 19-year-old me—light in her eyes, fire in her heart, still hopeful in spite of the chaos around her—wouldn't just fail to recognize this version of herself... she'd mourn her. A hollow shell dressed up in expensive clothes and painted-on smiles, pretending to be a woman in control when, in reality, I'd become an echo of someone I used to be.

By the time we got home that evening, my body was begging for rest. My heels had conspired with gravity to try and break my will. I'd spent hours laughing at jokes that weren't funny, sipping overpriced cocktails while silently counting the minutes until I could shed the costume and breathe like a human again.

But peace never came quietly in that apartment.

The second we stepped through the door, the mask dropped—his mask.

"Why do you always look so tired and disheveled?" he asked, dripping venom like it was foreplay. "You embarrass me in front of my friends."

I blinked, stunned, but not surprised. That was the thing—eventually, the emotional punches stop feeling like attacks and start feeling like routine.

"I'm just tired," I tried to explain, voice calm, like I could logic my way out of his mood. Rookie move.

"Tired? You're always tired," he snapped. "Maybe if you put more effort into your appearance, you wouldn't look so pathetic."

Pathetic.

It hit harder than the slap that would come later. That word lodged itself somewhere in my chest and rattled around like a loose screw. But I didn't fight back. I didn't cry. I did what I had trained myself to do—I walked away.

I made it to the bathroom. Sanctuary. At least that's what I hoped.

I turned the water on and started scrubbing off the evening like it was a bad decision I could wash down the drain.

Then came the footsteps.

He was behind me before I could brace myself, his anger spilling over like he was addicted to it.

"Don't walk away from me when I'm talking to you!" he bellowed, grabbing my arm so hard I could feel the bruises forming in real time.

I froze.

That moment—the split second before a storm hits, before the first clap of thunder—it hung in the air. Heavy. Dreadful.

And somewhere deep inside me, that 19-year-old version of myself—the one who swore she'd never let anyone treat her like this—screamed.

But she was muffled by fear.

By exhaustion.

By survival mode.

"Look at you," he said, his voice suddenly calm in the most chilling way —like the eye of a storm, quiet just before it wrecks everything in its path. "You're nothing without me. Remember that."

If this were a movie, this would be the line that echoes hauntingly later, when the protagonist finally escapes and reclaims her power. But in real life, you don't get dramatic music cues. Just silence, and your own heartbeat sounding like a warning siren in your ears.

Now, I hadn't yet learned the ancient wisdom that "a soft answer turns away wrath." No, I was still in my clap back era—armed with sarcasm and just enough buried resentment to ruin the mood.

So of course I said it.

"What are you talking about? You wouldn't even be living in this nice apartment if it wasn't for me."

And it was true. Legal issues had blacklisted him from just about every landlord's good graces. No lease would touch him. No utilities in his name. I was the signature on everything. The foundation of the lie. The illusion of stability he used to keep up appearances.

What I didn't know then was that this setup would bite me hard two years later. After I left, I'd have to threaten legal action just to sever ties with the electric company—because somehow, this man had bribed employees to keep the lights on in my name while racking up a secret $4,000 bill. A sort of reverse magic trick: now you see financial freedom, now you're in debt.

Still, I didn't regret saying it. I never have. But the timing? Yeah... could've been better.

The slap came in slow motion, like a bad soap opera scene. I saw it coming—had a full second to move, flinch, something—but I stood still.

And then crack, left side of my face, direct hit.

Oddly, it wasn't pain that struck first. It was insult.
The pure audacity of it.
He slapped me. He actually slapped me.

And then we just… stood there.
Frozen.
Wide-eyed.
Like two actors who forgot their lines in the middle of a live performance.

Eventually, he released my arm and walked away, like he hadn't just torn a piece of reality off its hinges.

I stood there holding my cheek, heat rising under my skin, not from pain, but from the humiliation of being someone who got slapped and stayed. I turned toward the mirror, slowly, almost afraid of what I'd see.

The girl staring back at me looked like a stranger cosplaying as me.

Big, beautiful curls—but too dark now, too unnatural. Brows arched with surgical precision but still a little too thin, like they were trying to disappear. Her wide eyes were full of something I couldn't name—fear? Disbelief? Grief?

It had to be another girl.
Some poor thing I should feel sorry for.
Someone I should try to help.
Because surely, that couldn't be me.

But it was.

And in that moment, I understood the line had been crossed. This wasn't just verbal warfare anymore. This was a new battlefield. One with bruises.

And something in me shut down.

I didn't cry.

I didn't rage.

I became numb.

You can't hurt me if I don't feel anything at all.

Right?

The days that followed bled into each other like watercolors left out in the rain. I drifted through them like some half-formed ghost, haunting my own life. My senses were dulled—like someone had wrapped my brain in bubble wrap and forgotten to pop it for relief. The city, once a vibrant chaos of endless possibilities, now resembled a maze designed by someone who hated people and was into psychological warfare.

Traffic buzzed, people talked, dogs barked at things that didn't exist—none of it registered. Everything was background noise to the static in my head.

One evening, after yet another argument that ended with me feeling like emotional roadkill, I found myself on the balcony. The city lights flickered below like a thousand tiny lies pretending to be stars. The air was cool and smelled faintly of rain and urban despair. Inside, the apartment was heavy with the kind of silence that only follows yelling and the slamming of doors. I stood there, arms wrapped around myself, breathing in the quiet like it was the last clean thing left.

And then—out of nowhere—a memory surfaced. A flash of my younger self, full of piss, vinegar, and a wildly unjustified belief that I could handle anything. That girl was fearless. That girl wore eyeliner like war paint and thought heartbreak was just another plot twist. She had dreams. Colorful, stubborn, loud dreams. And somewhere along the way, I'd traded her in for someone smaller, quieter—someone who tiptoed through her own life trying not to upset anyone, especially him.

That was the real betrayal. Not his—mine. The moment I stopped standing up for myself wasn't loud. It was slow, like erosion. But it gutted me all the same. Realizing that you betrayed yourself is a different kind of heartbreak.

The next morning, I woke up with a weird, unfamiliar feeling: clarity. It tasted like bitter coffee and revenge. I started making plans, quiet ones, stealthy as hell. I reached out to old friends—the ones I ghosted not because I didn't care, but because it was easier to disappear than explain. I called my mom, who answered on the first ring like she'd been waiting for it. Piece by piece, I started stitching together the safety net he'd convinced me I didn't need.

The day I left felt like skydiving with a parachute I packed myself—equal parts terror and adrenaline. My hands shook as I zipped up my bag, every creak of the floorboards sounding like a potential plot twist. I stepped outside and the world didn't end. It actually smelled…nice. Like exhaust fumes and freedom.

Ironically, I realized I'd outgrown "Numb" by Linkin Park—the song that used to feel like my personal anthem. Now, it was R. Kelly's "When a Woman's Fed Up." A problematic bop, yes, but the vibe was on point.

I took a deep breath, and for the first time in a long time, it didn't feel like a performance. The past was heavy, but it was behind me. The future? Unclear. But at least now it was mine to mess up on my own terms.

Still, freedom has a twisted sense of humor.

He didn't let go easily. Men like him rarely do. For months, he clung to the ghost of our relationship like it owed him something—showing up at my job, lurking near my apartment, watching me with the desperate eyes of someone who couldn't believe he no longer had control. Every time I saw him, it felt like a jump scare I hadn't agreed to. I lived in a permanent state of survival mode—high-functioning fear in a decent outfit.

The first time I knew I was being stalked was after a late-night shift. I was driving home, already exhausted enough to question if I'd hallucinated the burnout on my left headlight. Then I hit a police checkpoint—routine, except nothing about that night was routine. As I rolled to a stop, heart thumping like I owed it money, a car pulled up beside me. It was him. Cool as ever, he walked up to the officers and said, "She's with me." They let me go without another word—because he used to be one of them. That moment was more than chilling—it was a masterclass in how systems fail women in slow motion.

After that, paranoia became my sidekick. I changed routes home like I was in a spy movie. I slept with a bat next to my bed—not that I knew how to swing it with any real threat, but the fantasy helped. I didn't live, I just navigated threats.

Then came the day I saw him outside my building. I was already emotionally bankrupt from work, and there he was, leaning against the wall like a bad plot twist. My heart did the now-familiar somersault of dread. I thought about turning around, but some awful part of me wanted closure—or maybe just proof that I wasn't imagining the hell he'd dragged me through.

As I tried to walk past, he stepped into my path. Predictable.

"What?" I asked, my voice barely more than a breath.

His eyes scanned me like he was searching for the version of me he used to manipulate. "I just want to talk," he said, voice soft, like he was auditioning for empathy.

I stared back, face blank. I had no anger left to give—only numbness. Years of anxiety had turned me into a grayscale version of myself. If he was expecting fire, all he got was ash.

He flinched at my silence. "What happened to you?" he asked, like I was the tragedy here.

I didn't respond. There was nothing left to explain. The silence between us screamed louder than any words I could offer.

He stood there for a moment, just… looking. Then something flickered in his face. Realization? Regret? Gas? Hard to say. But his posture sagged like a balloon losing air. "I'm sorry," he whispered, like it changed anything.

I didn't believe him. I didn't care enough to correct him. I just wanted to be left alone.

He took a step back, the bravado gone. "There's no more hope, is there?"

I shook my head once, slow and deliberate. He nodded like he'd known the answer all along but needed to hear it anyway. Then he turned and walked away.

I didn't chase him. I didn't watch to make sure he was really gone. I just stood there, letting the stillness wash over me. The city lights blinked around me, uncaring and alive. The night air kissed my skin—cool, crisp, merciful.

And for the first time in what felt like forever, I didn't feel like prey.

I felt... okay. Not euphoric. Not healed. But okay. And in the wreckage of my old life, that felt like a damn miracle.

I walked into my apartment and closed the door behind me. Not with fear —but with finality. The future was still a giant shrug—but it was mine. And that tiny spark in my chest? That was hope, reintroducing itself after a long hiatus.

That night—and well into the next day—I slept like the dead. Not the poetic kind of sleep, either. I mean coma-level, don't-wake-even-to-pee kind of sleep. My body, after years of being stuck in fight-or-flight mode, finally waved a white flag. It was like my mind, my muscles, even my bones had finally whispered, It's safe now. And so, I let go.

When I finally opened my eyes, sunlight was spilling gently through the curtains, painting the room in warm golds and soft shadows. For the first time in what felt like forever, I didn't wake up bracing for something. There was a strange stillness inside me—not empty, just... quiet. Like a fog had lifted, and I could finally see myself clearly again.

Rebuilding my life wasn't a dramatic montage with uplifting music—it was slow, intentional, and sometimes awkward as hell. The first real step? Reaching out. I called my sister. Her voice, thick with love and just the right amount of judgment, wrapped around me like a weighted blanket. She didn't hesitate to tell me how I'd changed—how I'd become someone unrecognizable. A mannequin, she said. Perfect hair. Perfect posture. Giant handbag surgically attached to my arm. The kind of woman who declined chairs like sitting down was an act of war. She said it with a laugh, but it broke something tender open inside me.

That call reminded me I wasn't alone. I never had been. I'd just forgotten how to ask for help.

In the days that followed, I turned to reading and writing—two old friends I hadn't seen in years. I devoured novels, self-help books, celebrity recommendations, and the entire Oprah book club like it was a survival kit. The stories—real and imagined—became mirrors and maps. As fictional women clawed their way through fictional hells, I felt like I was clawing my way out too. The smell of paper, the sound of turning pages —they were a kind of therapy that didn't require me to speak.

I wish I could say that the Bible brought me through—that it was scripture that steadied me, that I flipped through Psalms like a warrior of light. But no. Back then, it was fictional heroines and memoirs of messy rebirths that held me up. I was a woman of faith—but at that moment, my faith wore different clothes. Sometimes it looked like an underdog in chapter twelve finally standing up for herself.

And then there was writing. What began as scattered words slowly took shape. With every sentence, I uncovered a version of myself I thought I'd lost. The girl who saw meaning in quiet moments, who spilled her emotions onto the page—she hadn't disappeared. She'd just been waiting for a moment that felt safe. Each paragraph felt like a rescue mission. And with every page I wrote, I felt a little more whole.

Healing doesn't follow a script. Some days I feel like a phoenix, rising from ashes. Other days, I feel like a raccoon in emotional recovery— sleep-deprived, slightly feral, and trying to do my best. But every tiny victory counts. Every step forward is proof: I survived.

I'm not running yet. Hell, I'm not even walking gracefully. But I'm crawling in the right direction, and that matters. Healing, it turns out, isn't about erasing the past—it's about proving to yourself, every damn day, that you're more than what happened to you. And like a river slowly carving its way through stone, I'll keep moving forward. Not perfectly. Not quickly. But with purpose. Because I'm still here. And I'm not going anywhere.

# *RISE*

The best way to love SOMEONE is to inspire them
To become the best version of themselves
In a world filled with so much hate, suffering and despair
Where can we find such love?

It is within you

Even in your darkest of dark moments
When you feel you have no more to give
Absolutely nothing left
You still have love
Always love

The darkness - how cold and suffocating
The obscene lies it tells
Crushing our Dreams and our Hope
Makes us believe there is no escape
Getting through requires remembrance

Remember the light
Remember where it is
Remember that no matter how many raging storms
blow past you
Or how many dark and dense clouds linger above you
The sun NEVER stops shining
If we rose above the clouds
We would feel the sunlight on our faces

So let us rise
And continue rising above

Rise above that unkind word
Rise above that loveless act
Rise above that mother or father that abandoned you
Rise above that person you depended on to protect you
Rise above that one who betrayed you
Rise above that pessimist that didn't and still don't believe in you
Rise above that friend who keeps disappointing you
Rise above all the people that you ONLY wanted to love you
Rise above that insecure, fearful voice inside your head constantly
doubting you
And keep rising
I promise that you can always find the light
Because it will always find YOU
The light always returns because it is only
The darkness that is temporary
Love is Light
Light is Love
You were borne from love TO love

The best way to love YOURSELF is to become convinced
Of an eternal truth....that you are
WORTH IT
Be light
Be love
Rise.

# Being Redesigned

IT FEELS LIKE breaking.

The way the ground shifts beneath you. The way the walls you built so carefully start to crack. The way pieces of yourself that you thought were permanent suddenly feel provisional, temporary, like they were never meant to last this long anyway.

You're supposed to hold it together. That's what you've been taught. Keep your shape. Maintain your form. Don't fall apart, don't come undone, don't let them see you crumble.

But what if falling apart isn't the failure? What if it's the first honest thing you've done in years?

You're not being broken. You're being redesigned.

There's a difference, though it doesn't feel different when you're in it. Breaking is violence—something shattering under pressure it was never meant to withstand, something destroyed beyond repair. But redesigning? That's intentional. That's necessary. That's what happens when the blueprint you've been following no longer fits the life you're trying to build.

You outgrew yourself. And now the old architecture has to come down to make room for what's next.

Think about how a bone heals. It breaks, yes. But in the breaking, the body rushes to the site with everything it has—cells and minerals and fierce determination. It doesn't just patch the crack. It reinforces it. The bone becomes stronger exactly where it broke. The fracture becomes the foundation.

That's what's happening to you, even if you can't see it yet.

The parts of you that are dissolving right now—they weren't wrong. They were right for who you used to be, for the smaller room you used to live in, for the person you were before you knew what you know now. But you can't unknow things. You can't unbecome. You can't crawl back into a skin you've already shed.

So the redesign begins, whether you're ready or not.

Maybe it started with grief—a loss so large it rearranged your understanding of what matters. Maybe it started with betrayal—someone you trusted showing you that trust itself needs redesigning. Maybe it started with success—achieving the thing you thought would complete you, only to discover the emptiness on the other side.

Or maybe it started quietly. A whisper that became a hum that became a roar: *This isn't working anymore. This isn't me anymore. I can't keep being this anymore.*

And now you're here, in the terrifying middle place where the old is gone but the new hasn't fully formed. Where you don't recognize yourself in the mirror because you're between versions, suspended in the space between who you were and who you're becoming.

This is the hardest part. The waiting in the rubble. The not knowing if you'll ever feel solid again. The nights when you lie awake cataloging everything you've lost—the certainty, the identity, the story you told yourself about who you are and how life works.

But look closer at what's actually happening.

You're not collapsing. You're shedding. You're not fragmenting. You're sorting—keeping what's essential, releasing what was only ever borrowed or forced or built to please people who don't even live in your house.

You're being stripped down to studs so you can be rebuilt on a foundation that's actually yours.

The redesign doesn't ask your permission. It doesn't wait for a convenient time. It doesn't care if you're ready or if you understand or if you'd rather stay the same, thank you very much. It comes when the gap between who you are and who you need to be becomes unbridgeable. When the old model can't take you where you need to go.

And yes, it hurts. God, it hurts. Because you loved some of those old pieces. Because you worked hard to become that previous version of yourself. Because tearing down anything—even something that's outlived its usefulness—feels like destruction when you're the one being demolished.

But you're not the building. You're the architect.

And the architect knows something the building doesn't: this isn't the end of the structure. It's an expansion. A renovation. A transformation from something that was fine into something that's necessary.

You're being redesigned to hold more—more truth, more complexity, more capacity for both joy and sorrow. You're being redesigned for a larger life than the one you were living, even if you can't see the blueprints yet, even if right now it just looks like mess and dust and nothing where something used to be.

The person you're becoming needs different rooms. Bigger windows.

Stronger walls in some places, no walls at all in others. Space for things the old version of you couldn't have imagined wanting: radical honesty, deep rest, fierce boundaries, soft vulnerability, the ability to hold two contradictory truths at once.

You can't add those to the old structure. The old structure was built for someone else's specifications—your parents' dreams, your culture's expectations, your younger self's understanding of what safety looks like. It worked then. It doesn't work now.

So it has to come apart. Not all at once, maybe. Not necessarily with drama. Sometimes the redesign is quiet, almost invisible from the outside. But internally, everything is shifting. Load-bearing walls are being moved. The foundation is being examined. What was once the center is now off to the side.

And you—you're learning to trust the process even when you can't see the outcome.

This is faith, though not the kind they taught you. Not faith that everything happens for a reason or that there's a plan you can't see. Just faith that you're tougher than you thought. That you can survive your own transformation. That whatever is being built inside you is worth the demolition of what came before.

You're not being broken.

You're being broken open. Being remade. Being expanded into a form that can hold all of you—the parts you've been hiding, the parts you've been denying, the parts you didn't know existed until pressure forced them to the surface.

And one day, when the dust settles and the new architecture stands, you'll look back at this moment and understand: this wasn't the end.

This wasn't the end. This was the beginning. This was the part where you stopped being built by other people's hands and started designing yourself.

On purpose.
From scratch.
With everything you've learned about what you actually need to thrive.

The breaking?
That was just the demolition phase.

What comes next is the building.

As you turn the final page, I want to share something personal—
something I wasn't always ready to admit, even to myself. Not
all, but most of the pieces in this book are rooted in my own life.
The moments of clarity? Real. The healing? Ongoing.
Some of these pieces were like little lifelines I threw to myself
when I was in dark, confusing, or just plain messy seasons of life.
Spoiler alert: sometimes they worked, sometimes they just made
me want to cry in public.

Life has this uncanny ability to throw curveballs—usually when
you're already juggling three flaming swords. But somewhere
between the chaos and the quiet, there are these small, powerful
moments. Moments that remind us we're still here, still healing,
still growing. That's what I tried to capture here: not perfection,
but progress. Not tidy resolutions, but honest reflections.

I won't pretend I've figured it all out. I still trip over the same
lessons occasionally (*okay, often*)
But writing these pieces helped me stand back up, and maybe,
just maybe, they'll help you do the same.

If anything you read here made you feel a little less alone, a little
more hopeful, or even just made you laugh at how wildly
unpredictable life is—then it was worth it.

Thank you for walking this road with me. Be gentle with
yourself. And remember...
**broken pieces can still find peace.**

I Appreciate You,

*Serenite*

# About the Author

Serenite Hope is a writer who believes that nothing human can ever be alien to us—which explains why she's spent years excavating the messy, uncomfortable, beautiful parts of being alive, turning them into words, then into books so you don't have to feel alone in your weirdness.

**Whispers of Healing** is her author debut, but it won't be her last whisper (or shout) into the void.

If you connected with these pieces, you'll want to explore **The Human Series**—a collection of raw poetic essays, lyrical meditations, and social commentary that says all the things we're told to keep quiet. **Every Shade of Human**, **this too, is human**, **a little too human**, and **still, somehow human** are self-deprecating, painfully funny, and achingly real. They're love letters to our contradictions, our chaos, and our refusal to be anything other than gloriously, messily human.

And if you're craving stories that feel like living inside someone else's heart for a while, check out **Between Breath and Breaking**—a book of cinematic short stories told in first-person narration, where every character is trying (*and sometimes failing*) to survive themselves.

When she's not writing, Serenite is probably deep in a Chinese drama spiral (because Mandarin is the most beautiful language in the world, *obviously, fight her*), asking "but why though?" about literally everything, or wondering how other people manage to be normal when there's so much to feel and think and say about being alive.

She writes because some truths are too stubborn to stay silent.

And because if we're all walking around pretending we're fine, someone has to be honest first.

**Connect with Serenite Hope:**

**Website:** www.riseliftingothers.com
**Blog/Newsletter:** serenitehope.substack.com

www.ingramcontent.com/pod-product-compliance
Lightning Source LLC
Chambersburg PA
CBHW060126130626
46556CB00006B/2248